SCIENCE AND HUMAN VALUES
IN THE 21st CENTURY

SCIENCE
AND
HUMAN VALUES
IN THE 21ST CENTURY

Edited by
RALPH WENDELL BURHOE

THE WESTMINSTER PRESS
Philadelphia

ISBN 0-664-20907-6

LIBRARY OF CONGRESS CATALOG CARD NO. 74-146667

BOOK DESIGN BY
Dorothy Alden Smith

Published by The Westminster Press®
Philadelphia, Pennsylvania

PRINTED IN THE UNITED STATES OF AMERICA

Contents

Maybe 6

Preface

The Pittsburgh Theological Seminary, as part of its 175th Anniversary celebration in 1970, convoked some three hundred scholars, clergymen, and laymen to contemplate the implications of the startling advances in science and technology for human values. As the vast and inexorable clockwork of the calendar approaches the end of the second and the beginning of the third millennium of the year of our Lord, many of us have been wondering about the destiny of man. The changes in the human situation since the year of our Lord have been tremendous. But the most of this change has come about at an accelerating pace in the past 175 years since the seminary was founded. The reason: the impact of the revolutionary advance of science and technology. In 1800 there were no computers, atom bombs, or television; no cures for poliomyelitis, diphtheria, or malaria; no airplanes, automobiles, telephones, radios, or steamships. Jumping over the moon could be conceived of only as an optical illusion. Railroads and household stoves were just being developed. The population of the world was about a quarter of what it is now, and it took more months then to travel around it than it does hours today. Today we can talk and send pictures to Australia in less than a second, whereas then it took many weeks. People on the American continent hardly imagined what was west of the Mississippi River. The few who had some dim notion of people living in such places as China and Japan thought of them as we might think today of living foreign beings on a distant planet—hardly of any practical concern to us.

Today we are more than three billion interdependent, but badly organized, potentially very unstable, people crowded into Spaceship Earth. Scientific knowledge has provided machinery that is increasingly taking over not only the hard labor and the skilled labor, but has, in the past twenty years, begun to take over the clerical, management, transport, communication, educational, and even planning and decision-making functions of men. Not only is the scientific technology changing the circumstances and meaning of human life, but the new scientific notions of the nature of man and his place and meaning in the world have been transforming our attitudes in these past 175 years. Then, Bishop James Ussher's Biblical chronology was the ground for supposing that the earth had come into existence less than six thousand years ago, whereas now we read the creation story of the earth and the life upon it in terms of a few thousand million years. Our "myths" concerning man's origins, his place in the scheme of things, and his destiny are very different from what they were in 1800. Scientific knowledge as well as technology is changing our faith in our traditional values.

Thus, added to the uncertainties and fears resulting from our now being immediately threatened by massive populations who seemingly do not share our values and who are fast attaining equivalent capacities to utilize the same fantastic technological powers, our own faith about our own tradition and in our own meaning and destiny has been eroded. Increasing numbers of our population, especially the later arrivals, are dubious about the values handed them by our tradition. Many openly reject them. It seems that our society is falling apart from within as much as it is threatened from without.

What, then, about human values in the twenty-first century? This was the question posed by Pittsburgh Theological Seminary's 175th Anniversary Committee. This book presents an edited and somewhat expanded version of the response to this question. The seminary's committee, under the general chairmanship of President Donald G. Miller and the specific chairmanship (for this particular symposium) of Director of Continuing Education William P. Barker, invited the following men to contribute to this book. All but Dr. Mowrer participated in person in a three-day session in Pittsburgh, March 11–13, 1970.

Ralph Wendell Burhoe, author of Chapters I, II, VII, VIII, and the Epilogue, is Professor and Director of the Center for Advanced Study in Theology and the Sciences, and Editor of *Zygon, Journal of Religion and Science,* at Meadville/Lombard Theological School, affiliated with the University of Chicago.

Harold K. Schilling, author of Chapter III, is a physicist and University Professor at Pennsylvania State University.

Langdon Gilkey, author of Chapter IV, is Professor and Chairman of Theology at the Divinity School of the University of Chicago.

O. H. Mowrer, author of Chapter V, is Professor of Psychology at the University of Illinois.

Robert L. Sinsheimer, author of Chapter VI, is Professor of Biophysics and Chairman of the Division of Biology at the California Institute of Technology.

The faculty of Pittsburgh Theological Seminary and a large number of distinguished scientists and scholars from numerous schools as well as clergymen and laymen attended the symposium as formal and informal discussants and critics who sharpened and refined the thinking of the major speakers.

I was asked not only to write extra chapters but to edit the volume. I gratefully acknowledge the critical encouragement and assistance of my wife, Calla, and the skillful assistance of my secretary, Rachel Davis, in this task.

R. W. B.

Chicago, Illinois

CHAPTER I

Prophesying Human Values

Ralph Wendell Burhoe

The Call to Prophesy

We have been called to be prophets, to prophesy concerning human values in the future. There are two major meanings of the term "to prophesy": (1) to foretell the future, let us say in the twenty-first century; and (2) to speak for God or to reveal sacred truth. In these essays we are called not merely to predict the future but also to say something about the ultimate meaning and concerns of human life in the face of drastic changes which many suppose will soon be upon us, that is, to reveal sacred truth about human destiny. Either form of prophecy is risky business. Humiliating are the failures of science and technology to predict such a common physical system as the weather very far in advance. But to pretend to represent and to interpret the future on behalf of the ultimate determiner of human destiny, that most complex phenomenon on earth, this would seem to be utterly foolhardy, an act of vanity and pride or stupidity that would seem bound to be smashed.

Yet, as will appear in these essays, man, in fact all life, is a future-predicting system. Predicting and adapting to the requirements of the future are the very essence of living, even though the bulk of our predictions and attempted adaptations turn out to be failures. Perhaps the first and most important thing we can say about our nature is that it is our destiny to try to prophesy—to try to discern what is sacred for us and to predict future circumstances so that we are prepared to adapt to them as may be required in order to maintain what is sacred about our life.

Korzybski's phrase that man is a time-binding animal[1] is one that has caught our attention and has intrigued us in the twentieth century when the various sciences of life are revealing the ways in which this time-binding does take place. When one celebrates the past of a theological school or anything else, one is really planning for the future. Memorials and memories are guideposts for future orientation. Life today and tomorrow is built from a pattern of memory, the remembered cumulated learning in history of what makes life possible. The memory of past experience encoded in the DNA molecules of man's (and all earthly life's) genetic heritage is the sacred key for continued life, for the renewed life of the next generation, and the base on which all improvements of life must be built. The memory of past experience encoded in the brains, the behaviors, and artifacts of human cultural heritage is the basis for the continuity and advance of human civilization. For example, the primitive society's memory of the sun god's program for springtime as a time for planting seeds is a necessary element in an agricultural technology. The memory encoded in an individual's brain of his life's experience of rewards and punishments by brothers, parents, and gods is the basis for his plans for his next move. Memories at all levels of life are representations of past history which are selected for their usefulness as a code or key for what one must do to maintain or advance life in future history.

The very possibility of memory means that in the phenomena or events to be remembered there is something that does not change, something that remains invariant amid the flux of time. If a pattern was not perceived at least once before, it cannot be said to be a memory. Fundamental to memory is that patterns of the world—and also their reflections in a living system's adaptive responses thereto—recur in essentially the same form, either continuously or intermittently. Memory depends upon the stability or invariance of some characteristics of reality.

Life itself is a memory, a something that continues to be the same thing in the midst of a flux, like the constant shape of the waterfall which is never twice made up of the same drops of water. The possibility of life depends upon there being some elements or characteristics in the surrounding flux that remain the same. The stability of certain already existing elements or aspects of the habitat is a part of the "memory" or "invariant pattern" that is necessary for life. Also the successive, potential, new levels of stability within patterns of evolving organisms are the ground for ever higher and more complex forms of adaptation to nature's requirements for the continuity of life.[2] Many of life's patterns in man have had a longer continuity or stability than the mountains and continents of the earth.[3]

Because life is a special kind of stable pattern that like the waterfall remains the same in the midst of flux, it must anticipate and regulate trends in the flux in order to maintain its proper pattern, or as biologists say, to maintain its homeostasis.

But man's time-binding from memory to prophecy and hence his planning for the future has had a very uncertain success. Historians and social scientists generally have been so badly bitten that they have eschewed theory and prediction, and have adopted a rule to focus on empirical, documentable facts of the past or on phenomena of the directly observable present. Such statements are less apt to be knocked down by contrary evidence in the future. The timidity or humility of the historians or social scientists to the contrary notwithstanding, a contemplation of the scientific picture of man suggests that the whole purpose of memory of past events is to anticipate or predict future events so that we may adapt ourselves to the future, to the impending requirements for life.

In any case, there is no dearth of prophets for the future and in particular for the second millennium. It must have been about a decade ago (at which time I was the executive officer of the American Academy of Arts and Sciences) that I began conversations with my late friend, Lawrence K. Frank, on the possibility of an Academy commission to try to think ahead to the dangers and opportunities for man that a rapidly changing science and technology would bring about by the year 2000, and what therefore we need to anticipate or prepare for. The commission was set up, and its first published reports came out in the issue of *Daedalus* for the summer of 1967 entitled "Toward the Year 2000: Work in Progress."

In the past few years there have been numerous other conferences and even semipermanent institutions established, along with a flood of articles, books, and even new journals, seeking to portray the possibilities and dangers of the new millennium. Along with technology and politics, religion and values of the future have been considered, including such books as *Religion in the Year 2000*,[4] by Andrew M. Greeley, and *Values and the Future*,[5] edited by Kurt Baier and Nicholas Rescher.

The essayists of this present volume were convoked to attempt to prophesy in this latter area, that is, to prophesy not only about future circumstances but in particular about those future circumstances that are most sacred or of ultimate concern to man. Commonly man's ultimate or most sacred concerns or values are called his religious values, and our prophecy here should attempt to reflect the second meaning of prophecy, as I have said—to reveal sacred truth.

How Is Prophecy of Future Events Possible?

But now to return to the problem of prophecy in its meaning of "foretelling," "prediction." I come out of an experience in a science whose task is the foretelling of the future of a fairly simple physical system, the earth's atmosphere, that is in some ways much simpler than the systems we call life or human culture. My early career was in meteorology where physics was applied to prophesy or foretell the weather. Even with the arrival of widespread observations of the atmosphere and the computations of electronic computers, there is still great difficulty in forecasting weather even a day ahead, and the reliability of the forecast for a specific atmospheric pattern falls off rapidly for each day farther ahead. If such a simple system as the physics of the atmosphere is so difficult to prophesy a few days ahead, how dare we talk about the condition of that unpredictable piece of nature called humanity or human values as much as a few decades ahead?

Capacity to predict a system's behavior depends on finding some relatively simple (comprehensible) and unchanging (invariant) relationship between the state of the system and time (its historical transformations). This relationship may be expressed in a formula such as "The sun rises every morning," which may be translated to a more elaborate formula such as "The sun circles the earth regularly" (Ptolemy's model) or "The earth turns on its axis regularly at the same rate so that every twenty-four hours the sun will be highest in the sky again at noon" (Copernicus' model). We have found this a pretty invariant formula of a system's relation to time and hence the system is highly predictable.

We can extend our capacity to predict by finding other factors in a separate system that are regularly or invariantly *dependent* on (determined by) some factor in a first system for whose succession of states in time we have already worked out invariant formulations. For instance, we know that in many places on earth the temperature is highly dependent on the amount of radiation coming in from the sun. Thus, for these places, we can safely predict that it will be warmer tomorrow at midday than at midnight. Such predictions are about as safe or reliable for the year 2000 or the year A.D. 2,000,000 or the year 2,000,000 B.C. as they are for tomorrow. We can safely predict when we can formulate a reliable invariance with respect to time in one element of a system and a reliable invariance of dependence of other elements of the system on elements whose time dependence has already been successfully established. By looking for such reliable statements of invariance as the rotation of the earth and a relatively simple dependency statement (such as the dependency of the temperature above a piece of earth on the position of the sun), we can make fairly certain statements or prophesy far ahead (or backward) in time.

Much simpler organisms than man can make such predictions and behave accordingly, as do the deciduous trees that know when to prepare to send out their leaves in the springtime. The genotypic DNA memory of single-celled protozoa can predict and prevent the internal manufacture of certain molecules above or below the proper numbers advantageous to the life of the cell. We can also make some statements about humanity that are about this simple and this sure. One of them derives from the rather simple dependency of people on energy from food, and hence our security about the prophecy that the human population is limited by its food supply. We can further give fairly close estimates of limits on levels of food supplies, and thus say with a good deal of certainty that if we do not otherwise limit the population below such levels, the food supply itself will limit it to that level by the starvation of whatever number is in excess. By such search for invariances and simple dependencies, we can prophesy about many things human. Of course, the invariant entity may not be obvious, and often is found only after a long search.

We would be foolish to base predictions merely on present trends, whether these be present trends in population growth or in temperature change. No one would be alarmed if some enthusiastic measurer of the atmospheric temperature in the spring came to us with the empirical evidence that the mean temperature this week was two degrees warmer than that of the previous week, and that that was warmer than that of the previous week for the past five weeks, and then declared that at this rate of increase it would soon be so hot that we would all be roasted to death in hell by next February. We already know that we can't allow this temperature observer to project his trend ahead on a straight line, since we already know that the annual orbit of the earth is such that by the first day of summer the sun, on which this temperature depends, will start its decline in all latitudes of the earth more than the summer solstice latitude from the equator.

Our problem in prophecy is to find an invariant element or relationship in our conception or model of the part of the world that we are trying to predict. In the temperature phenomena just described the real invariance is not the increase of the average temperature each week, but the annual tour of the earth around the sun, all the while keeping its axis tilted just the same degree from the plane of its orbit. Until you have found what is truly invariant in a system you cannot do very well at forecasting or in adapting your life in such ways that you can prosper in relation to it.

I want to point out that man, when he began his search and conjectures concerning the ultimate causes of events a long time ago, began searching for invariants. An ultimately invariant principle of the cosmos was formulated before the Christian era in some such terms as "that reality which is eternal, unchanging, all prevailing; that reality on which all things, including human life, depend." One might say that the first formulation of an invariance principle was made by the formulators of theological symbols. The Psalms have some lovely portrayals of a reality, more invariant than the eternal rock, that guarantees our security and our future.

One might raise here the question as to whether any and every search for an invariance principle is theological. As everyone knows, the philosophers of Athens were searching for invariance principles at the same time the psalmists were writing, and we in the West are heirs to some of the mixtures of metaphors from Judaic and Greek sources about the ultimate and unchanging Prime Mover or ground of all being. And we also know that the natural philosophy or science of the past few centuries inaugurated, in the search for invariance, the more systematic use of a criterion for validity, the test of empirical, observable confirmation in addition to the older tests of the philosopher-mathematician: logical coherence. Incidentally, it has been suggested by some scientists[6] that it was the convergence in one culture of the Greek claim for the power of logic with the Judaic claim for the power of historical or empirical fact (objectivity) which gave modern science its birthplace in Christendom.

In any case, by the time of Galileo and Newton we find the formulation of new laws of invariance, such as Newton's laws of gravity and of planetary motion, which have such universality that we can predict planetary events—for instance, the exact time of a lunar eclipse, forward and backward for centuries with great accuracy. Most people are not aware that Einstein's so-called law of *relativity* is actually a law of *invariance,* and some scientists have suggested that "law of invariance" would be a better name for it.[7] Einstein was also responsible for another formulation of invariance that made a single system out of what were formerly two separate and independent systems of invariance: the conservation of mass and the conservation or invariance of energy. In the celebrated statement $E = mc^2$ he represented the fact that in any transfer between the realms of energy and mass the exchange involved a constant or invariant equal to the square of the velocity of light. The energy derivable from the mass of the system invariantly equaled its mass multiplied by this large constant, c^2. I shall return later to how the revelation of these and many other scientific statements about invariances underlying the phenomena of our world may be related to the earlier theological formulations of eternal verities. But first I want to indicate more fully the relation between life (or life's values) and prophecy.

Life's Values and Prophecy

In my first few paragraphs I mentioned that life and prediction are very closely related, and that memory or some principle of invariance (whether in genetic DNA, in nervous systems, in cultural artifacts, or in the environing nature or habitat) was the basis for the behavior of all living systems in maintaining themselves (homeostasis) by adapting to changing conditions. In short, a viable memory is one that allows the cell or organism or society to respond (to predict and to adapt) appropriately to a whole range of future contingencies in such ways that it will remain alive, in being. Such a memory is not just any accidental remnant of a past experience, but a very special remnant of many past accidents that has been selected because of its power to predict with a remarkably high degree of probability just what must be done in the midst of a very uncertain, turbulent, disturbing world in order to keep the living self in its rather delicate but necessary good order. I think we shall find that such memories, such accumulations of information, are the grounds of values.

One of the grand revelations in recent science of an invariance in nature is the statement first formulated by Darwin more than a century ago that the varied and wondrous forms of life "have all been produced by laws acting around us."[8] From a wide variety of forms produced, natural causes weed out the "less-improved forms" in numberless small steps, in such a way that all the complex patterns of life were evolved from primitive forms. A century later we have traced back in time and space the operations of these natural laws, so now we see life evolving from and selected by the matter and energy of the world and the cosmos.[9] This may be logically akin to the story which said we were all descended from Adam and created by God, except that today our story is much fuller and better documented.

Moreover, the evolutionary or Darwinian statement makes as clear as does the religious formulation of more than two thousand years earlier that the supervision of human progress did not stop with Adam but continues to the present moment.

It may be said that natural selection is daily and hourly scrutinizing throughout the world, every variation, even the slightest; rejecting that which is bad, preserving and adding up all that is good; silently and insensibly working, whenever and wherever opportunity offers, at the improvement of each organic being in relation to its organic and inorganic conditions of life.[10]

Interesting is how close this picture is to that of Ps. 139:

O Lord, thou hast searched me, and known me. Thou knowest my downsitting and mine uprising; thou understandest my thought afar off. Thou compassest my path and my lying down, and art acquainted with all my ways. . . . Search me, O God, and know my heart: try me, and know my thoughts: And see if there be any wicked way in me, and lead me in the way everlasting.

Whether we read Darwin's scientific picture or the psalmist's, they are both statements about an invariant, inexorable supervision over good and evil in all life or behavior, preserving the good and rejecting the evil. This notion of an order-producing, life-building selection by sources transcending the evolving train of living organisms has been largely overlooked by humanists and the general public in their interpretations of the scientific revelations about man's evolution. Much of the feeling of meaninglessness of contemporary youth and the secular world is erroneously blamed on supposedly scientific notions of the inhospitability of the universe to man, or notions that man is a freak accident who has to contend with and defeat nature. But a careful reading of the best authorities will give a very different picture. George Gaylord Simpson reflects many other contemporary evolutionary theorists when he says: "Natural selection is no random or chance process, but quite the contrary. It is directional and directive, and it must lead precisely in those adaptive directions that have in fact characterized the course of evolution."[11] We could say that natural selection is the name of the processes of nature by which those innovations (random or non-random) of patterns of life, which happen to be better adapted to or stable in a particular environmental niche, do in fact remain in being, while other competing patterns, which are not in fact so well adapted or stable in that niche, do in fact tend to disappear. The fact that natural selection is often selecting from random variations is true enough, and this makes the story that natural selection produces living systems of ever-increasing order all the more wonderful.

In the past couple of decades, the theory and supporting evidence have extended this picture of evolution back into a period that preceded any structures we could ordinarily call living, into earlier periods of chemical and cosmic evolution. Here it is being shown that processes inherent in the nature of the cosmos are operating to bring into being structures or states that nature prefers all the way up through successive levels of organization from hydrogen, through the periodic table of elements, to complex molecules, to living systems of molecules, to human life. So certain are many scientists about the universality or invariance of this scheme that we fully expect to make contact with other sentient beings in the cosmos, possibly by the twenty-first century.[12]

For two reasons I have briefly introduced some of the invariances about the nature of life (such as our kinship with all life back to a common ancestor and with the basic processes of cosmic evolution) and the invariance of the process of the selection of life at all levels. First, I wanted to remind you that we have some invariances on the bases of which we can understand and explain and make some prophecies about living systems, including ourselves and our value systems. Second, I want to give a little more detailed background for my next statements about why we men are creatures who inherently require a vision, certain goals for the future, or a system of values, and why we inherently need to be prophetic about future conditions of ourselves and our world. I want to demonstrate that the cosmos ordained man to prophesy, and I am here underlining both meanings of prophesy: (1) to predict the future and (2) to reveal the will of God for man as a living being.

The Role of Replication and Cybernation in Values

In order to understand the intrinsically prophetic nature of man, it is helpful to ask quite carefully what is the nature of life, and how it is related to what I said earlier about memory. Contemporary science is finding it hard to draw any sharp line between the living and nonliving aspects of nature. The same physics pervades dust and men, and we can properly say that out of the dust was man made. But we do distinguish living bodies of dust from lifeless ones. I want to focus attention on two characteristics of physical systems that are involved in those we call living species, whether amoeba or man: *replication and cybernation.*

Replication of new generations is produced by a memory or inheritance, a coded or symbolic design of what is essential, what is of value, for reconstructing or regenerating a living cell or organism of the same general design as the parent. It should be remembered that a living system or being is a very complex arrangement of molecules, very complex compared with the patterns they have when they are only the dust of the earth. So the memories that keep the design and then replicate these complex patterns of life are very complex memories. Yet, living organisms have this capacity to make very accurate copies or duplicates of this complex code of their basic design. In recent years we have learned that the code is written in an alphabet of deoxyribonucleic acid molecules whose structure we have discerned and which we call by its acronym or initials: DNA. In this recent chemistry we have begun to learn something very significant about *memory* of living patterns and its replication *as a part of* the physical cosmos, *not as something alien to it.* It is important for us to know that this memory—which is duplicated or replicated in the processes we call procreation and which is "read out" by a special ecological niche in the generation or growth of a new being of the same general pattern—is a very precious and rare, in fact, very improbable and very complexly designed or highly informed, pattern of things. The order, organization, or meaningful design of the arrangement of a portion of the string of DNA in your genotype, let us say a million DNA long, is just about as rare and improbable as your finding a million-letter sequence of the Bible or a scientific text coming out of a shaking hopper containing a million letters that were allowed to drop on a moving belt.

The memory or pattern of arrangement found in the molecules of living beings, while it is produced by ordinary physical processes such as those which operate in water and dust, involves a very special arrangement of those processes so that what has been learned over the passage of thousands and millions of years is preserved. We have considerable capacity today to explain this preservation system in terms of the nature of the molecular bonds in DNA, in terms of the double-helix, duplicate-strand, or die-mold character of the genetic memory, and in terms of the copious and extravagant manufacture of copies that allows the natural selection process to weed out fatal mistakes or errors in the copying process.

But the main things to keep in mind are, first, that the complexity and rarity of living organisms is encoded in a sacred memory of more than a thousand million years of trials and errors which have been selected or judged for their capacity to maintain and permit the enhancement of the living process; and secondly, that this memory is memory about the self and its relation to its natural world, because the selection process that winnowed out the errors is the outcome of the interaction between the living systems and the natural world. Life and its replication through its sacred memory is itself an invariance phenomenon in the scheme of things.

You and I are thus constituted and come into the world with this marvelous heritage of values which structures the capacities of feeling, sensing, and behaving that are characteristic of us and hence endow us with our unique kind of life. I will say some more later about how our human culture and civilized ways are related to this same cosmic program of creativity by trial and error always winnowed by a selection process that in Darwin's words "is daily and hourly scrutinizing . . . every variation, even the slightest; rejecting that which is bad, preserving and adding up all that is good."

But first we need to move beyond the marvels of memory in projecting life's future by replication to that other feature of life important for understanding prophecy's role in life and life's values, and this is *cybernation*. Cybernation means the governance, regulation, control, or maintenance of some characteristic or quality or goal. A fundamental property of all living systems is that, when anything—either from their environment or even from inside them—disturbs or disorders their pattern of life, then they repair themselves, they restore the order, they maintain a constant pattern in spite of events that tend to disturb it. Man has learned to make nonliving machines that will do this, like a swing or a pendulum which will tend to hang straight down again after you have pushed it away from the direction of the plumb line. Such nonliving machinery with norms or goals also exist in nature even before life was created, such as lake levels that are generally maintained within certain limits in spite of variable rainfall, so that there is nothing in this cybernetic or self-directing or self-governing characteristic of life which is alien to the cosmos revealed by physics.

But the cybernation of self-governance or purposive action of living systems, like their memory systems, has been increasingly enhanced in the evolutionary series by several stages of newly emerged levels that have been selected in life's evolution from the more simple to the more complex patterns of viability or stability. Nature has selected successive refinements of the basic physical designs of the self-regulating systems of life, systems that maintain (remember) their specific patterns against disturbances of various kinds that threaten to destroy them. In all living systems (from single cells to complex human organisms to still more complex human societies) their vital characteristics are maintained against lethal disruption by systems of control which maintain the norms or goals of the living system within the necessary limits. Such systems of control in biological organisms are usually called homeostatic ("stay the same") mechanisms. A term that is equally applied to man-made and to natural homeostats is "cybernetic" mechanism.

Whatever the name used, these cybernetic mechanisms involve the following features which are exemplified in a thermostat or temperature-control mechanism, such as the one that keeps your room temperature or your body temperature within certain specified limits, norms, or goals.

First, there is a "remembered" goal, a range of temperature within which the room, refrigerator, or body must be kept. In our bodies, this memory is supplied to the homeostatic mechanism in the brain by the genotype or genetic heritage. In the thermostat on your wall the "memory" of the goal or desired temperature is supplied by where you set the dial, perhaps at 70° Fahrenheit.

In addition to this remembered information of the basic goal or value that it is desired to attain, there must be information predicting temperatures that may exceed the limits set as the normal or desired values. That is, the homeostat must be able to predict or prophesy a future state. If the future predicted will be too warm, then the heat source must be shut off; if the future predicted will be too cool, then the heat source must be turned on. The thermostat makes this prediction by the fact that the thermometer which an instant ago registered a temperature within the remembered limit or goal range now registers a temperature higher than that limit. This is a prediction that unless the heat source is shut off the temperature will go too far above the limit.

In addition to (1) possessing information about the desired value or goal and (2) receiving information predicting the trend beyond the goal limits or bounds (too high or too low), the homeostatic or cybernetic mechanism must be able (3) to steer or control the source of heat so as to avoid future states beyond the limits of the desired or necessary values. In the thermostat on your wall, there is a wire that goes to the furnace to operate the switch that turns the furnace on or shuts it off. If the furnace is producing so much heat that the thermostat predicts that the norm or goal temperature will be exceeded, then the thermostat, by means of its own electric switch that is actuated by the temperature change, sends what is called a "negative feedback" to the furnace, a signal or piece of information which effectively says "stop, quit, don't send so much heat" by switching it off.

Thermostats are one kind of homeostat. Homeostats in living systems are mechanisms or ways by which established goals or patterns of stable, living order may be maintained in spite of the threats to disrupt them that come from irregularities or disordering forces.

The same principle of cybernetic or homeostatic mechanism operates in the bodily organism to control the temperature of mammals, and in human markets to control the manufacture and supply of goods. A living cell, or organism, or human society can be characterized as a complex of interacting networks of homeostatic goals or norms or purposes, usually integrated in some hierarchy that makes certain generalized goals or values more valuable and in which each of the lower-level goals or values is organized to subserve the higher-level goals or values.

By such homeostatic mechanisms all kinds of living systems maintain their normal states. It must be remembered that living systems are by their very nature homeostatic systems, systems that maintain themselves, systems that on the whole are not destroyed by accidents and changes of circumstances. This is their purpose, their goal, to remain in being, to stay alive.

One should not be misled to think that life fails because it is an empirical fact that all living creatures that are observed long enough die. In the scientific picture of man, as some of the great religions have long maintained, some inner core of the reality of each living being does not die. Today we have good evidence of the nature of a complex strand of the inner core of our being that has been in being and in the process of evolving or development continuously as far back in time as we can survey. Scientists have begun to make even clearer than has religious poetry why the death of the temporary body is both necessary and good for the growth of man's sacred and lasting form of being which we may properly call his soul. The homeostatic system which we call life transcends the lifetime of the individual body and even the lifetime of a species. The fact that our genes for cytochrome C are continuous, with but slight modifications, back for millions of years before *Homo* emerged in evolution is testimony that homeostasis of the dynamic patterns of our life is not frustrated by death.[13] Our basic being as revealed by the sciences is not necessarily interrupted by the death of the body.

In the scientific revelation concerning the nature of man, we have found that the human brain has a population of cells greater than the population of people in the world, and we have found that inside each of these cells there is a machinery more complex than that in a large manufacturing plant carried on by a highly complex and dynamic program of billions of molecules. It is also known that this highly ordered and complex machinery, made of the same molecules that make up the dust of the earth, carries on both of the major processes of living systems to which I have referred: memory or replication and cybernation or homeostasis. The brain contains in each cell a replica of our genetic memory or genotype, most of which is many thousands or millions of years old.

But the brain also contains a new kind of memory, a kind that corresponds to the way we usually use this term, the memory of what happened a minute ago, a day ago, a year ago, and for some of us, several decades ago. In the brain most of this new memory recorded in our lifetime is not any more available to our conscious awareness than is our genetic memory. The psychologists have referred to this (plus the genetic memory) as the "unconscious." But a modest portion of what has happened in our personal history we can recall to consciousness, and a modest portion of the present moment's input to our nervous systems is available to us as patterns of which we are immediately aware or conscious.

In the past few decades, a most significant field of the scientific world has revealed how the brain—with all these kinds of memory of past events, including a genetic and cultural memory of our goals and purposes—also carries on the major direction of our homeostasis or cybernation as if the brain were a supplement to the genotype in this. That is, the brain is the physical locus that directs our behavior to fulfilling our goals including our capacity to move, eat, love, kill, talk, and write, and underlies our consciousness or awareness of feelings, sensations, perceptions, willings. Our very goals themselves (to eat and drink, to hunt and harvest, to keep warm and love, etc.) are written or remembered in our brains. Our goals (in which term I include wishes, purposes, norms, values) are specified in our brains' homeostatic settings.

The brain also receives the new information predicting future needs and contains the cybernetic feedback or motivational mechanisms that operate to maintain or fulfill these complex hierarchies of purposes. The brain or central nervous system is the central coordinator or cybernator of a tremendously complex hierarchy of nets of values, goals, or purposes received as inputs from genetic, cultural, and personal experience that characterize human life.

A brain acts not only as an integrator of the individual organism but also of the total culture and society.[14] There is as yet no human culture or social organization that is either remembered or governed without involving brains. It is true that our cultural artifacts, including especially our libraries, provide important and essential coded information that brains can read out; but the cultural-technological library is as dead without a brain to read it out as is the genetic information coded in the DNA dead without the cell protoplasm to read it out.

Research on the brain is being carried on by many disciplines from physics to psychology. They are finding close parallels in the living brain to the homeostatic mechanisms I have pointed to earlier as being characterized by (1) information on goals that is registered in memory, (2) information mapping present trends and predicting any deviation from the proper goals, and (3) means for operating controls to prevent the deviation from going too far.

The brain has these three features. (1) Information from the genetic and newly learned memories of what is required (the goals, norms, values, wishes, etc., necessary for life) is found registered in the inner core of the brain which also activates our basic feeling states. (2) Information from various parts of the organism and from the environment on the current state of things and current trends is fed through various channels for analysis largely in the outer and back portion of the brain and also for comparison with the goals specified in the inner core. This is necessary for the production of our awareness of ourselves and the world about us. (3) At this point the information from (1) and (2) is fed into a computer or prophesying section of the brain which seems to involve heavily the frontal lobes in relation to the core in order to predict the kinds of actions necessary to satisfy the goals.

These latter activities of the brain seem to underlie our feelings with respect to the future—our hopes and fears, our values. In "hopes" or "fears" the brain circuits are switching to operate controls that will maintain the self in well-being, maintain values. This last homeostatic action might include the unconsciously turning on of the sweating to keep cool, with consequent conscious thirstiness and drinking. More elaborately (but not always more effectively for the accomplishment of the same limited goal yet possibly providing a wider satisfaction of many other goals simultaneously), the brain may initiate a long chain of behavior that has been learned perhaps from family experience, including asking Dad for a ride to the lake, the taking of bathing suits, friends, and all the activities connected therewith.

The brain's computer, predicting certain present and future conditions and possibilities, becomes a decision maker. Conscious awareness and thought parallel neurological factors involved in such decision-making. Some of the structures and mechanisms of the brain in producing the memory of goals, the new information and predictions of needed adjustments, and finally the consequent decisions necessary to maintain life are partially revealed by this rapidly developing area of the sciences, as a look at the literature already cited and a vast related literature should indicate.

We have suggested that life may be described as a cybernetic or homeostatic mechanism, that is, as a system that has learned how to maintain and enhance its complex, delicately balanced, internal nature even when its immediate surroundings are producing disturbances that would degenerate it quickly if the living system did not know how to (have the information and will to) respond appropriately to keep itself in being. We have seen that such behavior requires prediction, or prophecy, of future circumstances if it is to be able to respond to them to gain the resources it needs for living and avoid the disruptions that will kill it. We have seen that the brain involves genetic and traditional cultural information about goals which it relates to new information about the self and its world as that is received through the sense organs; and that the brain integrates a complex world of information of various kinds and various levels (from molecules to stars) about how to live; and that the brain prophesies future needs or values and organizes the decisions that produce behavior necessary in order to maintain or enhance life.

We also pointed out and cited some of the literature that indicates that the brain is not only the central organizer of individual life but also of social life. It is the brains around the chief of state or at an international peace conference or at an industrial or scientific meeting that are hopeful or alarmed about the state of things and about the prognoses they make for the morrow. It is brains that make decisions to preserve or enhance the living social groups be they nations, economies, business firms, or families. This, too, is the function of brains in the religious institutions of society: to draw on traditional information about ultimate goals or basic feelings, to relate that information to information about the present state of affairs, and finally to prophesy and proclaim what man must do if he is to be saved.

I have perhaps come now full circle in my picture to indicate that prophecy as prediction about the reality on which our fate depends is an ancient program that has been carried out not only by the brains of Old Testament prophets but by the brains of men and donkeys and by more primitive prophesying devices going back in history for a thousand million years. I am trying to show that prophecy is the very essence of what any living system must do—a cosmic requirement that is invariant over a very long period. Therefore, it will be safe for us to predict that in the year 2000 our children and even we, if we are still alive, will be seeking to peer into the future of the reality in which we live, seeking to know what it says for our ultimate concerns, our basic values.

I might summarize some of the implications of these statements about the nature of memory and purposiveness (goals, values) by drawing your attention to the fact that life is an open (not rigidly structured, not completed) system or state of affairs, with a built-in purposive program to remain in being and to evolve further. The purposive program or goal is a very rare and special heritage or memory widely incarnated in DNA and in brains. This heritage enjoys a continuity of existence that far transcends the present moment and far transcends the lifetime of an individual man, and even far transcends the lifetime of the species. Here theologians can glimpse materials for credible doctrines of a soul's immortality. The cybernetic or goal-seeking mechanisms—informed by the memory, or the sacred heritage of life, and by current trends—operate to bring the general goals of the living system into being. Central to this goal-fulfilling are the sensing and responding operations of cells or brains concerning the internal norms, goals, or values and their relation to the present and future circumstances inside and outside the system as a result of changes taking place. Hunger is a prediction that the body is getting dangerously low on energy supplies, and smell may indicate where in the environment the needed food may be found. The same sort of thing operates at higher levels when "social indicators" observed by the social scientists or by a percipient religious prophet indicate that the behavior patterns of a society are inadequate for its viability unless the people repent them of their ways and behave more in accord with a standard required by real if not readily visible facts. The cybernetic principles and patterns are of the same general nature regardless of whether the internal reality is a cell or man or society and whether the external reality is water supply, or the attitudes and visions of neighbors, or some ultimate principle required of all living systems at all times.

I shall discuss the nature of the sacred, of sacred values and of religion, and of sacred prophecy concerning the third millennium A.D. in Chapter VII. Meanwhile, I shall turn to some of the more secular prophecies concerning the future of technology and religion. In Chapters III through VI we shall have the opportunity to look at the highly informed and serious views of three kinds of scientists and a theologian on various aspects of human values in the future.

NOTES

1. Alfred Korzybski, *Science and Sanity: An Introduction to Non-Aristotelian Systems and General Semantics* (The International Non-Aristotelian Library Publishing Company, 1933).

2. For a very insightful development of life's evolution from the molecular level through successive levels of stratified stability of increasing complexity in accordance with the laws of nature (including that second law of thermodynamics), see Jacob Bronowski, "New Concepts in the Evolution of Complexity," *Zygon, Journal of Religion and Science,* Vol. V, No. 1 (March, 1970).

3. The ancient patterns of some elements of the human genotype are discussed by George Wald in his "The Search for Common Ground," *Zygon,* Vol. I, No. 1 (March, 1966), p. 46, from which it is clear that basic elements of the genetic code of our essential Cytochrome C may be hundreds of millions of years old. According to recent geological theories, it was only two hundred million years ago that the present five or six continents of the earth were all part of a single continent in very different locations on the surface of the earth. This theory is popularly presented in Robert S. Deitz and John C. Holden in "The Breakup of Pangaea," *Scientific American,* 223:30 (October, 1970).

4. Andrew M. Greeley, *Religion in the Year 2000* (Sheed & Ward, Inc., 1969).

5. Kurt Baier and Nicholas Rescher (eds.), *Values and the Future: The Impact of Technological Change on American Values* (The Free Press, 1969); resulting from work over the past few years contemplat-

ing the time span "from the present to the year 2000," at the Department of Philosophy of the University of Pittsburgh.

6. E.g., C. F. von Weiszäcker, *The Relevance of Science: Creation and Cosmogony* (Harper & Row, Publishers, Inc., 1964); see especially p. 163.

7. Philipp Frank, personal communication.

8. Charles Darwin, *Origin of Species,* last paragraph.

9. Harlow Shapley, *Of Stars and Men* (Beacon Press, Inc., 1958). For a significant recent insight, see note 2, above.

10. Charles Darwin, *Origin of Species,* early in Ch. 4 on Natural Selection.

11. G. G. Simpson, *This View of Life* (Harbinger Book, Harcourt, Brace and World, Inc., 1964), p. 53.

12. Harlow Shapley, "Life, Hope, and Cosmic Evolution," *Zygon,* Vol. I, No. 3 (September, 1966), pp. 275–285, and *The View from a Distant Star* (Basic Books, Inc., 1963), especially pp. 55–74.

13. Wald, *loc. cit.* I add a word of explanation about my difficult paragraph on death and continuity. The evidence for the continuity of life's core patterns does not deny that much is destroyed. To help understand the continuity of the essential characteristics of life in spite of death, it may be helpful to contemplate the scientific picture that life is a pattern of flow, not a static thing. As a model, it may be helpful to picture life as the pattern of a waterfall. The millions of drops that constitute the waterfall now will have gone forever soon, but the waterfall remains. In either the scientific or the religious mode, one is not looking at the right thing if he defines the waterfall as gone if the drops have gone downstream or if he defines life as gone if certain molecules, certain cells, certain bodies, certain species have gone downstream. Readers will have difficulty accepting my statement "that in the scientific picture of man . . . some inner core of the reality of each living being does not die," unless they can accept it on faith or unless they can delve sufficiently deep into the scientific picture of man to understand how elements that characterized a man's genetic and other structures continue to circulate in the waterfall of life. "Inner core of reality" refers to that which is significant and which does in fact continue to circulate in the stream of life.

14. See, for instance, J. Z. Young, *A Model of the Brain* (Oxford University Press, 1964), in which he shows how the brain operates as the integrating mechanism in the complex homeostatic machinery of a living being. See also, for instance, Robert B. Livingston, "Brain

Circuitry Relating to Complex Behavior" in *The Neurosciences,* ed. by Gardner C. Quarton, Theodore Melnechuk, and Francis O. Schmitt (The Rockefeller University Press, 1967), pp. 499–515, who also points out the parallel function and complementation between the homeostatic mechanism of the genotype and that of the brain, and who also points out that we "must bear in mind that the brain is simultaneously the integrator of physiological, psychological, and social processes" (p. 500).

CHAPTER II

Some Prophecies
of Twenty-first-Century Technology
and Religion

Ralph Wendell Burhoe

Promises and Threats of Scientific Technology

There are many predictions about the fantastic technology of the twenty-first century, and some of the consequences for human values. These range from the destruction of life on earth by our technological power for overpopulation and ecological pollution, if not by nuclear energy, to the possibility of strange odysseys in space and encounters with life systems that transcend the human as we transcend the worm.

Predictions of paradise may be found in an infinite variety of possible and probable scenarios, such as that of a life of complete freedom and leisure for men provided by an automated economy that takes care of everything we need. The automated economy will even drive our cars for us safely on superhighways while we are drunk or drugged in heavenly bliss. It will provide us (every one of us, not just an elite group) with a wealth of gadgets for power and comfort beyond the power of the richest kings of previous ages even to dream. Our housing will be supertechnological and infallibly comfortable; even the world outside will be made perfect by weather and climate control if not by the more traditional technology of building a plastic dome over our residential and work areas. Technology will allow us to fly away to the moon and explore the planetary system at pleasure; or it will provide us with drugs and other euphenic devices that will open our minds and hearts and allow us to enter heaven right here on our pad. New pills or automated gadgets of one kind or another will perform the miracles to solve the population problem, the ecological pollution problem, even the problems of loneliness and unhappiness. Technology is our salvation. Such is the nature of some of the dreams or prophecies.

On the other hand, there are a good many evaluations and trends of technology which, if extrapolated, give us a less sweet picture of the year 2000. Some of these views include the trend toward overpopulation, which at least partially can be blamed on the "good" deeds of medical technology in the improvement of health and longevity. Then there is the forecast of the slow degeneration of the human gene pool, arising again out of a combination of religious and moral charity along with our medical technology, which preserves an increasingly larger portion of people with deleterious genes to procreate and eventually increase the proportion of the population that will be needing crutches, insulin, and all kinds of prosthetic devices and hospital care. This is different from the more immediate problem brought about by increase in the numbers of people needing such care produced by medical technology's capacity to keep already existing people breathing for longer and longer periods into age levels which they would ordinarily never reach. The genetic trend would increase the number of people who would need special and intensive medical care at younger as well as at older ages. Then there is the danger of overpopulation, which, together with the further kindly wish to provide each member of the population with more power and material facilities, will exhaust our resources, such as our fossil fuels, our raw materials, our water supply, the very oxygen we need to breathe.

Further dire prophecies include the uses, possibly by villainous dictators, of drugs and other technological inventions to brainwash a population so that it serves the establishment. It is said that birth-control pills and other devices of technology tend to break down sexual restraint and family loyalties, and by the year 2000 some predict a humanity engrossed in a wild orgy of immorality as a result of the leisure and other potentials made possible by technology. The fact that technology is now very rapidly bringing into the common pot of a single world society peoples who have been adapted to diverse levels and styles of cultural values may turn out to be not so much a melting pot as a pot that boils over or explodes. The confrontations of cultural values within formerly relatively stable population mixtures may spring out of a natural, unplanned, and inadequate human response to new technological and economic possibilities that may often be coming into effect too rapidly for any possible cultural or social integration, and too fast even for the prevention of disruptive explosions. The rapidity of the movement in the United States of the southern, rural Negroes to the northern, urban industrial communities is a confrontation of a population with a culture or social way of life to which it is not adapted. Cultures giving rise to different expectations of duty and privilege, when mixed too fast without time for proper enculturation, become explosive. The rising expectations, when combined with the often self-contradictory or self-defeating social or value structures of various peoples, may become tragically disruptive of human stability in the next thirty years and trigger a nuclear war, even if the Soviet Union and the United States were to continue their present programs of sufficient self-restraint and accommodation that have thus far prevented a nuclear holocaust. The potentiality of such a holocaust was anticipated or prophesied in the fears that haunted some of the physical scientists twenty-five years ago when they began to educate the political leaders of the United States and the Soviet Union why they should refrain from using or even testing atom bombs, and who were worried about the nth-country problem more than fifteen years ago. The nth is the name scientists are accustomed to use for designating some unspecified and as yet unknown one of a series; the nth country problem meant that some one of several possible countries which could become developers or users of atomic fission or fusion would have a probability of letting loose a holocaust, perhaps because it might not have a leadership capable of understanding the enormity of the tragedy or otherwise be capable of controlling the triggering of a holocaust.

Before we turn more specifically to values and religion, it is important for us to contemplate one special area of the already developing and the potentially fantastic technology of the twenty-first century that may have the most radical impact of all on human values. This is a rather recent technology that stems from a combination or teamwork of very sophisticated scientists of several sorts whose products are familiar under such names as automation, cybernetics, and computers.

It is important to consider the future of computer and cybernetic technology for human values because here we are witnessing the analysis and conceptualization in terms of mathematical logic of the very nature of what it means to be a goal-directed or purposive thinking and doing system. What is more, out of this new conceptualization is growing a vision not only of how to program an adding machine with feedbacks for self-control and purposiveness, but also of how the human being is similarly organized, and, what is truly terrific, also of how engineers may create "living, thinking, behaving, feeling, moral" machines able to do all we do before the biologists begin to synthesize something so simple as a biological cell. I have already noted that analysts of biological systems have observed that living systems are a kind of cybernetic or homeostatic computer system.

Intrigued with these potentialities, a prominent Swedish physicist, Hannes Alfvén, a few years ago under a pseudonym wrote a book entitled *The Tale of the Big Computer*.[1] To read it will give you a feel for how scientific minds can view the possibility of man's creating machines whose evolution in a relatively few decades could leave man behind. We do not have to worry about the scientifically rather poorly or negatively documented men from Mars or outer space that haunt the imaginations of a certain part of the public. But, the scientifically rather substantially documentable possibility that computers could by some time in the twenty-first century take on most of the functions of men, and perhaps all of men's ultimately valuable functions, as well as do many more things of significance for future evolution that organic men by themselves never could do, is something clearly before us. Before men confront their own computer "children" in their maturer stages, we should know something of the principles and values with which computers must be instructed or inculcated during their impressionable years, lest we have riots in the streets and oedipal or mechanical accidental slayings of the fathers. The generation gap that we now experience with our human children could become so wide between man and his computer child that we could readily imagine a chaos of destruction or a fantastic civilization as high above man as man is above the worm. In contemplating the possible superiorities of computers over men, what would be our understanding of human values? What are our ultimate concerns in such a situation?

In the motion picture called *2001: A Space Odyssey* and the book[2] you will see an imaginative and instructive view of an electronic computer called Hal whose morality and understanding seem to threaten his human companions. I am not certain what the artists of that picture wanted to convey in the end, and perhaps they felt the end was to present a problem. But as a prophet, I shall a bit later attempt to give you what I believe to be a more humane and a more divine prophecy concerning computers and men.

We could detail and document the probabilities of various pessimistic or optimistic projections of technological trends. We could report, criticize, and extend the growing literature in this field. But, because we are concerned with the future of man's most sacred values, we shall turn now from prophecies concerning various possible technological outcomes to prophecies about man's most sacred or religious values. First we are going to look at some of the recent predictions foretelling the future of religion.

Predictions Concerning Religion

First, we should note that in many of the current popular predictions of the future there is either no mention of religion or it is predicted that before the end of this century, according to some time scales, and before the end of the twenty-fifth century according to others, religion (which in such forecasts is often linked with "superstition"), not just God, will be dead. I can recall reading such prophecies by sophisticated predictors in my early years early in the twentieth century, and to quite an extent they have been right, although H. G. Wells's time scale may have been a bit fore-shortened. Among the more recent views are those of —James Allen Dator: "These functions [socializing the population] will be taken over by other social agencies. The Judeo-Christian religious establishment, as it is now organized or currently envisioned, is not likely to be one of these agencies. The Church is presently facing two challenges which may deal it fatal blows."[3]

In his book, *The Next 500 Years,*[4] Burnham Beckwith lists thirty-one major social trends, one of which is that "religious and superstitious belief and behavior have been declining for 500 years in most advanced countries and for shorter periods in all other countries. This trend is largely a result of the progress of science and education." He believes that the trend will continue and there will be a further decline in faith in ideologies, and that most of the world's adults will, by the beginning of the twenty-sixth century at least, be nonreligious and amoral (without religious or moral beliefs).[5] Less than 20 percent of the world population will attend religious ceremonies or pray at home. All governments and courts will strive to increase measurable welfare rather than to promote religion, justice, or morality.[6] One writer has suggested the future may provide "religiosity by pill ('consciousness expansion')."[7]

Herman Kahn, a noted if controversial predictor of the future, agrees with Beckwith concerning a basic long-range trend during the past several centuries. First in his list of trends is: "Increasingly Sensate (empirical, this-worldly, secular, humanistic, pragmatic, utilitarian, contractual, epicurean, or hedonistic) cultures." He contrasts this with such terms as religious, symbolic, worshipful, moralistic. However, he suggests that whether this [trend] will continue for the next thirty-three or sixty-six years is an open question. If the obvious implications of the description of the Late Sensate culture are valid, the long-term tendencies toward Late Sensate must stabilize or even reverse if the system [of culture] is not to be profoundly modified."[8]

Of course, there are predictions of a significant role for religion and church in the future, especially by men whose professional duty requires it. Thus, Krister Stendahl says, "It is unrealistic to believe that 'institutional religion' will fade away."[9]

Alvin Toffler, in summarizing the comprehensive University of Pittsburgh study entitled *Values and the Future,* states that "the organizers of this probe have gone out of their way to make it interdisciplinary. They have assembled economists, political scientists, philosophers, mathematicians, a businessman, a space engineer and others. Yet it soon becomes clear that, even so, they have not reached out far enough. Conspicuously absent from these pages are, for example, anthropologists, linguists, and behavioral psychologists, . . . psychiatrists, advertising men, market research and opinion research experts."[10] But nowhere does he mention the absence of theologians or clergymen. Obviously they can not be relevant for a study of human values in the future! I cite this omission of religion, church, clergymen, and theologians from one of the major current studies on human values and the future because I believe such omissions are typical and indicative of the status of theology and Christianity in many active areas of contemporary Western culture.

The doubt that Christian belief has any significant future (or even a present) is evidenced not only by its pointed dismissal by outsiders and by the even more damaging evidence that outsiders just don't consider it significant enough to mention even when talking about value problems, but the failure of religious belief is even asserted by a growing number of insiders. During the past half century an increasing number of clergymen have been quietly neglecting traditional doctrine in favor of a gospel according to Freud and related psychological, secular, doctrines of man and his salvation. In the meetings where professionals representing the theological doctrines meet with those representing the newer psychotherapeutic (soul-healing) doctrines, the discussion flows around the new psychological doctrines, even when they obviously violate the traditional religious doctrines. Traditional religious and theological doctrines of the soul and its salvation are seldom heard, unless outspoken fundamentalists happen to be around. The older religiously related tradition is increasingly forgotten, and the new secular psychotherapies are openly advocated by churchmen.[11]

Even in the heartland of theology itself, the key concept, "God," is declared dead. Langdon Gilkey in a penetrating analysis wrote: "Everything that our 'empirical' analysis of present church life has indicated, however, shows that this religious dimension has in large part dropped out of our denominational life, for much of the laity and the clergy alike. Issues of belief, of doctrine, or of behavior are no longer central or even real for our church life; and few seem to know or experience any religious elements in worship or in sacrament, or in personal life within the community of the church. . . . If religion as a word, and theological language as a mode of speech, point to the vertical, Godward dimension of the church's existence, then it is the disappearance of that religious dimension in our century that has in large part caused the irrelevance and unintelligibility of theological language about the church."[12] More recently, Gilkey noted that "whether . . . we look outside ourselves at intellectual movements in our cultural environment or inside at current changes in our feelings, attitudes, and convictions, we find religious concepts and certainties in upheaval, criticized not only by those outside the religious establishment, but even more by those within." Also, "today's theologian finds himself wondering whether he can do theology at all in the contemporary world. . . . This upheaval, this radical questioning of the foundations of religious affirmation . . . is now taking place *within* and not outside of the Church."[13] Peter Berger has suggested that "the 'crisis of theology' in the contemporary religious situation is grounded in a crisis of plausibility. . . . The fundamental problem of the religious institutions is how to keep going in a milieu that no longer takes for granted their definitions of reality."[14] In writing on "The Clergy in the United States," James M. Gustafson noted that there was a "breakdown of a sense of independent authority in the clergy," and that "in the absence of wide acceptance of the traditional bases of their authority, clergymen seek substitute ways to make themselves legitimate. . . . The American clergy . . . are no longer certain what their unique function is. . . . No matter what his faith and tradition are, the American clergyman stands between an ancient tradition and a culture in which God is remote, if not dead. This situation is felt to be a deep and agonizing crisis for many of the most sensitive and educated clergy. Consequently they are seeking those ways of work which will overcome the radical separation of religious life from the mainstream of the culture."[15]

The gloomy prophecies on the decline of religion from inside the churches are matched by studies from social scientists and the statistical samples of public opinion. *The New York Times* for March 5, 1970, carried a report on answers of persons in the United States to the same question asked by the Gallup poll on seven different Januarys from 1957 to 1970: "At the present time, do you think religion as a whole is increasing its influence in American life, or losing its influence?" The percentage who are saying religion is losing its influence increased from 14 percent in 1957 to 75 percent in 1970. *The Times* stated that "the reasons given for believing religion was 'losing' ground included these: (1) the church is 'outdated,' (2) 'it is not relevant in today's world,' (3) 'morals are breaking down,' and (4) 'people are becoming more materialistic.' " The report also said that these "findings represent one of the most dramatic reversals in opinion in the history of polling, according to the Gallup organization." Of course, church leaders and some of the people in theological schools in America have been aware of this potentiality, that the church is losing its influence in American life, long before the general public. I recall as typical a statement from a convocation of Roman Catholic bishops in the United States at the height of the post World War II back-to-church attendance boom, in which the hierarchy denied its significance for any real increase in religiousness.

The same disheartening facts for churchmen come out of the study by two sociologists, Rodney Stark and Charles Y. Glock, the first volume of which was published in 1968. This report concludes with an interpretation of the data reported. "The evidence leads us to two conclusions: the religious beliefs which have been the bedrocks of Christian faith for nearly two millennia are on their way out; this may very well be the dawn of a post-Christian era."[16] They found no health in either the religious orthodox or the liberals. They pointed out a lack of leadership, but added:

> However, leadership is not the only thing that is lacking. There is no clearly formulated theological and institutional alternative to provide the blueprint for renovating the churches. The critical attack on orthodoxy seems a success, but now what? The new theologians have developed no consensus on what it is they want people to believe, or what kind of a church they want to erect. . . .
>
> As matters now stand we can see little long-term future for the church as we know it. . . . This is hardly to suggest that religion itself will die. Clearly, so long as questions of ultimate meaning persist, and so long as the human spirit strives to transcend itself, the religious quest will remain alive. But whether or not the religion of the future is in any sense Christian remains to be seen. Clearly it will not be if one means by Christian the orthodoxy of the past and the institutional structures built upon that theology.[17]

These descriptions of the decline and predictions of the demise of religion from the human scene are discouraging and demoralizing to the religious institutions, their personnel, and to the wider public which, while not paying too much attention to detail, has supposed that morals and ultimate concerns were somewhere being kept in good order. There is certainly some truth in the reports of the decline and probably some validity in the predictions of the future. But I suggest we would be mistaken to conclude that religion had come to the end and was no longer to be a prime source of human values in the third millennium. One could properly make descriptions of the decline and predictions about the coming end of deciduous vegetation and insects every autumn, or in longer perspective about the vanishing of life generally just prior to each glacial advance. But, as I have already noted, life systems have strange and wonderful ways of maintaining themselves. There are such things as seeds and eggs that will hatch next spring and new species that will appear during climatic changes. Casual observers may fail to notice the true, often hidden, nature of the living system, and their predictions on the basis of only what is obvious are inadequate. I believe that many of the statements made about religion fail to deal with what is most essential. Since we still have not finished with some disheartening facts about human values and especially their presently perceived religious matrix, I want to assure the reader that I personally have full confidence in a new and flourishing era for religion in the third millennium, and I hope the reader will by the end of this book have a fair idea of why I say this.

The Metamorphosis of Religion in the Radical Reformation of Science

We are living at a change of season, in a time of the breakup of cultures. I am using "culture" as anthropologists use the term when they refer to the body of beliefs, behavioral patterns, and artifacts of a society of people—including the values or religious core of the culture that is involved in the motivation and regulation of characteristic goals and behavioral patterns. But I am prophesying that this decay and disruption of culture and its religious value core is to be succeeded by a reformation of culture whose dynamic core will be a reformed and universal religion.

I make such a prophecy on the basis of a doctrine of some perennial characteristics of human nature, characteristics that are drawn from various branches of scholarship about man from physics to anthropology and cultural history. My model on the basis of which I predict involves notions of a dynamic inner nature to individual, to societal man, and to nature in general and notions of certain impossibilities and possibilities which the ecosystem that created and sustains man demands of him if he is to continue in being. These make up the kind of boundary conditions and general laws of operation that I find are parallel to the kinds of predictions one can make as a scientist about some observable phenomena which have a history, like the topography of the earth, for instance. Anthropologists, historians of religion, sociologists, and others have noted that when man's situation changes radically so does his culture and his religion. In an evolutionary theory it is a matter of necessary adaptation. The philosopher Karl Jaspers in his *The Origin and Goal of History* has given the name "axial period" to approximately the first millennium B.C. He notes the critical changes of this period and the corresponding radical transformation in the great religious traditions, including those centered around the names of Buddha, Confucius, the Hebrew prophets, Socrates, Zoroaster, and with later developments associated with such names as Jesus and Mohammed. He and a number of others have suggested that we live in a similarly critical period and can expect similar radical transformation.

One prominent American theologian who also espouses this notion is Henry Nelson Wieman, who wrote: "By 'axial period,' I understand Jaspers to mean the most revolutionary turning point in the history of the human race. The first civilizations arose long before this time, developing in and around the first cities. But the period in history called 'axial' is given that name by Jaspers because at that time the moral standards and religious commitments came into being which made possible the subsequent development of civilization and culture."[18] Wieman adds that "just as agriculture and the city distinguished civilization from tribal life, so today the magnified power of scientific research and scientific technology distinguish post-civilization from the civilizations of the past."[19]

I share this reading of what appear to me to be pretty inevitable conclusions to draw about our historical situation. But, because ours promises to be a period of more radical change in the general culture, I believe it will produce a more radical religious change than that of Jaspers' "axial period." In 1958 I gave a statement of some reasons for this prophecy.

Whether or not one agrees with the particular analyses of any of the twentieth-century prophets of doom, such as the treatments by Spengler, Sorokin, or Toynbee; or whether one accepts seriously those vaguer adumbrations of despair, meaninglessness, and confusion being cast up profusely by sensitive artists and literati; there is a very simple bit of logic which lends ominous support to predictions of impending doom. This argument, which is supported by every area of empirical experience, is that when any particular order or arrangement of things is beset suddenly with a radically new set of forces, whether internal or external, that order or arrangement is placed under stresses that threaten its constitution. The more radical the new conditions, the more certain is catastrophe. And it makes no difference whether we are talking about an atom, a star, a prehistoric species, or a human civilization.

By uncorking the magic bottle of science, man has let loose a jinni which probably has more radically altered the conditions of human existence in the past century than anything that has happened in the past five thousand years; and it appears to be expanding its power to alter our situation at a rate which overwhelms our imagination to contemplate. I am referring now not so much to the releasing in the past century of a large part of the world's store of fossil solar energy that it took millions of years to build up, nor to the potential threats of the unleashing on earth of a vast, atomic nuclear type of energy like that which fires the sun itself, catastrophic though these may be; but rather I refer to the fundamental alteration of the pattern of the forces or conditions of life under which man for millennia has existed. To prosper under the former set of conditions, man's own internal design and controls have adjusted him, in response to the processes of natural selection since the beginning of life on earth. The threat to man is analogous to the threat to a species of fish occasioned by the drying up of the waters it had been inhabiting. Unfortunately for the fish, it did not have time to adapt itself to the ways of life necessary for survival on dry land, and there was no way it could get back to the watery circumstances for which it was adapted. It is very likely that man is not presently organized to survive in the drastically different environment he has unwittingly provided by his own technological powers.[20]

I must add a bit of interpretation to that quotation, so that it will not be supposed I am concerned only about the evolution of man's *genetic* structures by natural selection. In that 1958 paper, I used the term "natural selection," in what was then an especially unorthodox way, to cover the processes that select and reject all behavior patterns in molecular, organic, and cultural evolution. There should be nothing any more unnatural about the selection of the memory elements of man's personal and cultural nature than of his biological nature. But natural selection has tended to be a private monopoly of the biological evolutionists, and limited in its application largely to selection of what is now known as the DNA genotype, even though geneticists know that what nature selects is the phenotype or body and that the phenotype may be structured by information from the environment and culture as well as from the genotype. In man, in particular, it is known that the viability of organisms or phenotypes may depend very much on the culture type or patterns provided by the culture (such as dietary or sanitary and other culturally and not genetically remembered patterns of life) as well as on the genotype. Evolutionist Sir Julian Huxley[21] and others have recognized "ideas," "idenes," and other names for the units (analogous to genes) in which a culture type or total cultural heritage received by individuals is stored. Psychologist B. F. Skinner has even suggested that learning by behavioral reinforcement schedules is a "natural selection" process.[22]

It is only in the past decade or two that anthropologists and other psychosocial scientists have begun again, after a half century of avoiding it, seriously to use evolutionary models for the conceptualization of cultural history. It is well established that there are cultural as well as biological "species," "types," or "kinds," as for instance in the classification of languages. Languages are known not to be genetically but only culturally remembered. Cultural patterns are known to arise by random variations ("mutations") and are selected against or selected out because the society that bears them in its culture tends to disappear (that is, tends not to be viable) or because the society that uses them comes to prefer other patterns. Linguistics, again, provides good evidence.[23]

I am trying to say that from one scientific point of view we can understand that the total culturally structured pattern of a society (including its religion) may have been selected because it was well suited to guide the behavior of a people in adaptive ways under a certain set of circumstances. But the same cultural pattern may cause the societal behavior to be a frustrated fish out of water under some new circumstances, circumstances that in some cases may be brought about by the natural consequences of the earlier nature of the culture itself. One can say that the recent decline of Christianity is partially described by this model, if we grant with some scholars[24] that modern science is a by-product of the Jewish-Greek synthesis of Christianity, and with other scholars[25] that Christianity's God and hence Christianity was killed by the sciences. This situation, where a pattern that is good in one circumstance is bad in another, is also common in the genetic evolution of living organisms. Reformation processes are possible in both the genetic and cultural codes for living.

One big historical event of the present period as we move into the third millennium A.D. is that scientific technology is making the whole world of more than 3,000 million people smaller than a wilderness village used to be, so far as communication time and delivery time are concerned. You can talk or send a picture to someone on the other side of the world, say from Pittsburgh, Pennsylvania, to Canberra, Australia, and get a response in less time than you can get a response from someone a few blocks down the street by shouting back and forth. A bomb from an equal distance could be sent to wipe out the complete metropolitan area of Pittsburgh in less time than the fastest band of savage warriors two or three centuries ago could have moved over the less than twenty miles across Pittsburgh in a raid from a campsite say at Carnegie on one side of the city to another at Wilkinsburg on the other side.

The integration of human communities during the period between ten thousand and a million years ago probably customarily involved only some thirty to three hundred people bound by a relatively simple cultural tradition overlaying the natural biological bonds of an extended family. Such an integration by the Roman Emperor Constantine probably required providing bonds to coordinate and regulate a population of three hundred thousand human beings. The population to be integrated today is ten thousand times greater still. The billions of men today are clearly far more dependent on the proper behavior of one another than the relatively insignificant populations of the largest empires of the axial period of Jaspers. This immense crowd in the tiny village of Spaceship Earth is faced with the problem of integrating the values and behavior of at least enough of the leadership levels of the three billion people to provide mutual behavioral compatibility and stability, or else anarchy and destruction will make a mess of this spaceship village.

Not only has the world population reached an unprecedented number and crowding; reached a peak in the speed with which the communication of ideas, materials, and people can be shuttled over the face of the globe; reached unprecedentedly complex and stubborn problems of how to orient the tightly interdependent and yet huge masses of people in ways that are satisfactory, compatible, and viable too; and reached an incredible physical power per capita, which is equally capable of destructive as well as of constructive uses and which puts in the hands of individuals more fantastically destructive military power than was possessed by whole nations only a short time ago; but we have another unprecedented and still more threatening situation: there is no place to hide. There is no escape hatch for the survival of individuals or minorities who dissent from what they find to be noxious ways of their fellowmen. When the world was settled by small tribes, a dissident individual or group could slip away from the larger group whose values it felt were inadequate, and move to another part of the forest. Until the twentieth century there always has been some kind of place to which one could move, some possibility for isolation and starting over again in hopefully better ways. In Spaceship Earth such opportunities are decreasing by the decade, and are truly a bygone opportunity for most of us.

We do not have much time to find a stable, viable way of living together—much less time than the Roman Empire had, because the tempo of historical change has accelerated. Never in the thousand-year history of Greece or of Rome was there a step that compares in magnitude with the step in cultural evolution experienced by the whole world in the past century. The change in the ways of thinking and behaving, and the change in the magnitude of interdependence of people in the world has been in the past century fantastically greater than any comparable changes in the history of Greece and Rome over a whole millennium around Jaspers' axial period.

In this whole panorama of the twentieth-century predicament

of man, in the midst of all the unprecedented power, in the confusion of all the new complexities and ill-adapted, makeshift ways of providing human communities with the wherewithal to induce individuals to behave properly for the welfare of the total system as well as themselves, I find the crucial problem to be the lack of a currently credible and persuasive formulation of human values (goals, purposes, wishes, meaningfulness). At this moment in history there is evaporating from the minds of many young people, especially in the societies made affluent by technological know-how and power, the usual convictions of how a man's life is really as much bound by the necessities of the nature of things as it ever was in the past. But they do not see that bond and they do not in any case discern clear and convincing forms and rules that delimit the potentialities of their lives over and above the relatively feeble powers of magistrates, police, and presidents for maintaining or producing life's order. For these alienated young, the whim of the moment seems the best "reason" for whatever they do.

There are many other problems about finding a satisfactory vision of a man's private goals and their relation to the goals of society and the world; but this one of alienated people perhaps epitomizes the climax of the crisis of cultural and societal disorganization, and hence inability to function.

It is much akin to the disorganization of the insect organism when it is in the midst of metamorphizing or changing its structure and function from the wormlike pupal stage of life to a butterfly stage. The dynamics of human societies share with insect physiology, because of the capacities of human nervous systems or cultures to be restructured fairly rapidly, the capacity for environmental triggering of processes that may radically metamorphize or transform the character of the lives of individuals and the societies they constitute.[26] A change of jobs may sometimes involve as drastic a transformation of a man's character, habits, manners, disposition, etc., as a religious conversion.

But, in any case, the point is that before a metamorphosis can take place, the traditional templates that control the forms of structure and behavior in insects or men—as individuals or societies—have to become changeable and to be changed. The aimlessness of some of the alienated and the fickle changeability of others from one half-considered enthusiasm to another are characteristic of and necessary for a time of individual and social change. It is frightening to contemplate this unstructuredness and potential destructiveness if one does not also see some signs of a regenerating program to produce the new order; for certainly disorder is the same as death and defeat for all systems of life. We have basically the problem of the shaping of men's ultimate values, of men's religion, philosophy, morals, ethics, and all that gives to each individual the goals, vision, organization, motivation, habits, attitudes, aspirations, and courage that will direct his life in patterns that satisfy his own feelings, the needs of his fellowmen, and the requirements of the world.

If we look around in the world today, there does not seem to be any of the existing cultures which is possessed of a central value system that is able to permeate and integrate the three billion population of Spaceship Earth to give it an integrated, viable character. Even at home within the most highly civilized societies the value traditions are so eroded that it is common to find youth groups in universities who have abandoned the various older subcultures and have not yet found a new one that would appear viable. Such societies have more to fear from their internal weaknesses than from outside dangers. But the disjunction and lack of integration between the several different types of societies produced by different cultures and subcultures add to the confusion and increase the probabilities of misguided violence all over the face of the earth. Without any culture to provide the order and integration necessary for an interdependent population on such a complex and crowded technological spaceship, the probability of accidental destruction is increased.

If living systems are necessarily highly organized and integrated in order to adapt viably in an ecosystem, then it would seem clear that mankind's present state would call for some radical reorganization to adapt to radical changes in our ecosystem. Since it also seems that man is his own worst enemy in this situation; and not the climate, the soil, the forest, the beasts; it would appear that man has to be reorganized, reformed. In this crisis man's once effective beliefs about his ultimate goals, duties, and opportunities —beliefs carried by his traditional value system—now have become impotent to help him: partly because they are incredible, partly because they are irrelevant. But where will he find a value system that will organize him so that his life can be fulfilled? Will it be found by a breaking up of the present complex, technological civilization and a return to more simple forms? Will this require death and reduction of the population by some six out of seven people necessary to restore the world's population to the one seventh of the present population which a pretechnological civilization could support, say in 1650? Can we resurrect and return to the old beliefs the way they were? Can we find a way to advance, to move ahead to a revitalized religion for a new and possibly glorious age in the third millennium?

Fortunately, humans, like other populations, contain varieties of types. There is in human populations always the type of people who characteristically worry more, who see more dangers and fear more dangers, and who ferret out ways to overcome them. Sometimes this is combined with another type of character, the people who are concerned about the state of society, of culture, and of the institutions, and who worry about the dangers and threats to them, and who ferret out ways to overcome them. Sometimes these people are overly pessimistic and gloomy prophets of doom. Sometimes they have rosy-sounding messages of hope or even utopias. But from time to time, fortunately for the rest of us, they turn out to be right in their fears and hopes and they turn up with truly salvatory programs which provide the possibility of life for the rest of us. The ratio of "true" prophets to other prophets is probably about the same as the ratio of "would-be" inventors or creative artists to successful or "recognized" inventors or artists. If the number of disasters and threats in our world is increasing, we should expect that prophetism would be drawn out from more and more of those in the population who have that tendency and capacity within them. And we may, moreover, except that one or more will hit a bull's eye of significance for the society or the species. The authors of this book were convoked to this end.

Jaspers and Wieman suggested that we are now entering a new period for the advance of religion comparable to that of the first millennium before Christ. Certainly, if the historians and anthropologists are right about the transformation of religion as a part of the transformation of the general culture, we can expect that we may be entering such a period. I am convinced of it. I believe the present religious reformation will make historians of the twenty-fifth century think that in comparison the Lutheran reformation in Christendom of the sixteenth century was but a slight matter, and that the birth of Buddhism, Confucianism, Zoroastrianism, Judaism, Christianity, and Islam were only local preparations a couple of millennia earlier. One might say that the most important "technological" revolution at the beginning of the third millennium will be the greatest transformation yet in history of religion, of the operations by which men transmit the culturally remembered values from one person to another to provide salvation for the needs concurrently of the individual and of his society under the requirements of the ultimate powers. This will have to be a metamorphosis of religion that will integrate it with the ideas and facts of the new, one world of men living under scientific technology. I am more inclined to prophesy that we shall go ahead in this direction, albeit with some ups and downs and local upsets, than to disintegrate and to degenerate too far. While the latter is a real possibility, I am betting on the prophetic capacity given to man, by which he can far enough in advance properly fear what he must fear and love what he must love in order to maintain and advance this several-billion-year-old heritage of life on earth, and I have faith in the continuity of the source that created and nourished man's long evolving life that it will provide future opportunities.

In Chapter VII, I shall consider the nature of religion more carefully and present my prophecy of some elements of its revitalized and universalized world role in the third millennium A.D. But first we should consider how four other professors prophesy about human values and religion in the twenty-first century, especially as they are affected by science and technology. First a physicist, then a theologian, then a psychologist, and then a biologist.

NOTES

1. Olof Johannesson, *The Tale of the Big Computer: A Vision* (Coward-McCann, Inc., 1968).

2. *2001: A Space Odyssey,* a film produced and directed by Stanley Kubrick, with screenplay by Stanley Kubrick and Arthur Clarke based on a short story by Arthur C. Clarke (released by MGM in 1968). In the same year *2001: A Space Odyssey,* by Arthur C. Clarke, appeared (Signet Book, The New American Library, 1968); this was a novel based on the screenplay, accompanied by interpretative notes.

3. James Allen Dator, "Valuelessness and the Plastic Personality," *The Futurist,* Vol. I, No. 4 (August, 1967), pp. 53–54. This article was drawn from a longer paper entitled "Oh We Belong to a Cybernetic, Post-Money, Situational Ethics Society, My Baby and Me," a form of which appeared in the British architectural magazine *Archigram,* Spring, 1967.

4. Burnham Beckwith, *The Next 500 Years* (Exposition-University Book, 1968).

5. "The Next Five Centuries: A Prospective History Based on Current Trends," a review of Burnham Beckwith, *op. cit.,* in *The Futurist,* Vol. II, No. 5 (October, 1968), p. 89.

6. *Ibid.,* p. 87.

7. Nicholas Rescher, in Kurt Baier and Nicholas Rescher (eds.), *Values and the Future: The Impact of Technological Change on American Values* (The Free Press, 1969), p. 98.

8. Herman Kahn and Anthony J. Wiener, "The Next Thirty-three Years: A Framework for Speculation," *Daedalus,* "Toward the Year 2000: Work in Progress," Vol. 96, No. 3 (Summer, 1967), p. 708.

9. Krister Stendahl, "Religion, Mysticism, and the Institutional Church," *Daedalus,* Summer, 1967, p. 857.

10. Baier and Rescher (eds.), *op. cit.,* p. 27.

11. See, e.g., Ralph Wendell Burhoe, "Bridging the Gap Between Psychology and Theology," *Journal of Religion and Health,* Vol. VII, No. 3 (July, 1968), pp. 215–226; and O. H. Mowrer, *The Crisis in Psychiatry and Religion* (D. Van Nostrand Company, Inc., 1961).

55

12. Langdon Gilkey, *How the Church Can Minister to the World Without Losing Itself* (Harper & Row, Publishers, Inc., 1964), pp. 144–145.

13. Langdon Gilkey, *Naming the Whirlwind: The Renewal of God-Language* (The Bobbs-Merrill Company, Inc., 1969), pp. 7, 9.

14. See Peter L. Berger, *The Sacred Canopy: Elements of a Sociological Theory of Religion* (Doubleday Anchor Books, 1969), p. 156.

15. James M. Gustafson, "The Clergy in the United States," *Daedalus,* Vol. 92, No. 4 (Fall, 1963), pp. 724–744 (quotations from p. 724 and p. 731).

16. Rodney Stark and Charles Y. Glock, *American Piety: The Nature of Religious Commitment* (University of California Press, 1968), p. 205.

17. *Ibid.,* p. 223.

18. Henry Nelson Wieman, "Science and a New Religious Reformation," *Zygon, Journal of Religion and Science,* Vol. I, No. 2 (June, 1966), pp. 125–139 (quotation from p. 126).

19. *Ibid.,* p. 130.

20. Ralph Wendell Burhoe, in a paper entitled "Salvation in the Twentieth Century," which was published in Harlow Shapley (ed.), *Science Ponders Religion* (Appleton-Century-Crofts, Inc., 1960), pp. 65–66.

21. Julian Huxley, "Evolution: Biological and Human," a review of *Evolution and Man's Progress,* ed. by Hudson Hoagland and Ralph Burhoe, *Nature,* Vol. 196 (Oct. 20, 1962), p. 203. Also see Hudson Hoagland, "Science and the New Humanism," *Science,* 143:11 (Jan. 10, 1964).

22. B. F. Skinner, "The Phylogeny and Ontogeny of Behavior," *Science,* Vol. 133 (Sept. 9, 1966), pp. 1205–1213.

23. A good review and analysis of cultural evolution is to be found in Donald T. Campbell, "Variation and Selective Retention in Socio-Cultural Evolution," originally a conference paper in 1961 and published with minor revisions in H. R. Barringer, G. I. Blanksten, and R. W. Mack (eds.), *Social Change in Developing Areas: A Reinterpretation of Evolutionary Theory* (Schenkman Publishing Company, Inc., 1966); reprinted in *General Systems,* Vol. 14 (1969), pp. 69–85.

24. C. F. von Weiszäcker, *The Relevance of Science: Creation and Cosmogony* (Harper & Row, Publishers, Inc., 1964).

25. See Friedrich W. Nietzsche, *Thus Spake Zarathustra,* and the "God is dead" theme in recent theology.

26. The literature on religious conversion and the psychology of personality change provides much information on this topic, at the personal level, and history is replete with accounts of transformed societies. The following two books tie some of the psychological to the religious and social studies of the phenomenon: Anton T. Boisen, *Religion in Crisis and Custom: A Sociological and Psychological Study* (Harper & Brothers, 1955); Anthony F. C. Wallace, *Religion: An Anthropological View* (Random House, Inc., 1966).

CHAPTER III

What Is the Future of Man in the Light of the Challenge to Traditional Values?

Harold K. Schilling

Since no one knows or can know what the future of man will actually be, I assume that we are to consider what it could or should be—in terms of reasonable possibilities and expectations—from the viewpoint of my understanding of science and technology on the one hand, and of Christian faith on the other. Put this way the question seems to come from a stance of openness and from awareness that no answer can possibly be definitive or final, and this is the spirit in which I shall consider it. If, in the question, we emphasize the *should,* as I propose to do, it has the further merit of recognizing what has often been pointed out recently, namely, that man has entered upon that stage of his evolutionary development in which the future is not something to be predicted, but invented and constructed. What kind of world should we create, if we can?

Also, formulating the question in this way shifts the emphasis in our consideration of values from concern about the challenge *to* traditional values to concern about the challenge *for* new values. I dare say, the church, where it is at its best, is much more concerned with the challenge *of* the future than with the challenge *to* the past.

Now, as I present my thesis I would plead that it be regarded as an expression of hope and faith, not of cocksure certainty, as though the outcome were inevitable. I am *not sure* of the future.

I am, however, *confident*—by grace, I trust—about some of its general features. This confidence comes in part from what has been given me to know about the nature of man, of science and technology, and of reality. Most of all, however, it comes from my faith in God, who, as sensed so keenly by Paul (Rom., ch. 8), has unimaginable splendors in store for the world, and who, I believe, is using technology as one of his agencies for working out his purposes in it.

The thesis is that in the finite future man should, and can, become more fully human; and that in the 21st century he can take giant steps forward toward becoming the so-called "new integrated humanity" entering "the new world." We are moving even now from a world of men toward a world of Man. In this world of Man, men may well conceive and measure their selfhood and dignity in terms not so much of their *independence* and rugged individualism as of their *interdependence* and communal mutuality, and in which the individual person comes into his own only to the extent that he becomes an "individual in community," rather than an "individual unto himself." I have no illusions that this could be achieved painlessly, without terrible suffering, and horrible mistakes, and against demonically evil opposition; but it can be achieved, I believe, "with God," to use Dewart's potent phrase.[1] Please note especially that I have spoken of the coming of world *community,* not of a world collective, and particularly not of a governmentally imposed or controlled one. It is genuine world community that I suggest is possible. And one reason why it is possible is that man now has at his disposal science and technology.

Technology Is Transforming Human Values

Now, let us look at this thesis in some detail. My first observation is that right now technology is contributing mightily to an epoch-making transformation, not only of man's environment and physical existence, but of his mentality and behavior patterns, of himself and his value system. As Karl Jaspers, Marshall McLuhan, Walter Ong, and others have pointed out, this comes about at least in part as follows. First, "technology makes possible an enormous amplification of man's perception and apprehension,"[2] by means of instruments that functon as extensions of his senses, so that men must now be regarded as beings with a great deal of new intellectual, emotional, and spiritual capacity. Many hitherto unknown aspects and dimensions of life and reality are opening up to men. This is because they can now "see," understand, and appreciate much that was simply not available to them before. Second, they can now think more rapidly and effectively, and, what is more important, more holistically and mythically,[3] in patterns, and in depth, and more intuitively, and more sensitively "with their hearts," as well as minds. And they can participate, emotionally and with deep concern, more fully in the lives of other men—even at a great distance. Time span and distance have been virtually eliminated. There reigns now in human existence a global simultaneity of experience and perception. Third, these two developments are operating to bring men together into a world community of shared experience and concern.

What this means has been expressed incisively by Jaspers as follows:

What is historically new, and, for the first time in history, decisive about our situation is the real unity of mankind on the earth. The planet has begun for man a single whole. . . . [A] total metamorphosis of history has taken place. . . . All the crucial problems have become world problems, the situation a situation of mankind. . . . Nothing essential can happen anywhere that does not concern all. . . . *The history of the one humanity has begun. A single destiny governs the whole.*[4]

Surely, if this accurately depicts what is going on now, it "promises" for the future a truly humanizing development. Jaspers feels that to a significant degree this unity has actually been accomplished in its incipient stages, even though it is far from complete and ideal. He, and others, among whom I count myself, are fully aware of the devastating divisiveness, and competitiveness, and downright diabolical, shattering evil that is rampant in the world. Nevertheless, they see—just as clearly—that human individuals and groups *have* in our time been coalescing into a genuine, though far from perfect, global community, in which increasingly they work, play, and suffer *together,* and endeavor creatively to ameliorate evil and their common misfortunes *together.* In many areas of life we have already entered, though not very far, into a world in which interdependence, interrelationship, mutuality, and united participation in action are much more significant, and much more highly prized, than mere independence and untouchable sovereignty. Jaspers speaks of this phenomenon of unification, and the new mentality it represents, as the appearance in man of "a new consciousness of the world,"[5] and he considers it to be *the* development par excellence that is making possible the dawning of a truly new age in human history, and thus a truly novel emergence in human evolution.

Will Individuality Be Lost?

Unfortunately, this possibility—or probability—gives rise in the minds of many people to a great, and often almost paralyzing, fear—fear that in such a world of unified mankind the individual will lose his identity and individuality, and become simply a cog on a wheel of an inhumane, technologically dominated social machine. Without doubt the danger of this is very real. I submit, however, that it is not inevitable, as though decreed by fate. Consider, for instance, what we have come to understand about the concept of freedom, namely, that it means most when it is taken to signify not mere liberty, i.e., negative freedom *from* constraint, but positive freedom *for* mutually supportive participation in common creative tasks, and thus for cooperative achievement. We understand now also that such freedom can exist maximally and at its best only in a truly unified and integrated system of many entities and relationships, an organism that is more than simply an assemblage of loosely related, and essentially independent individual units.

Thus the process of worldwide unification, organization, and integration need not be an unmitigated evil. There is much to be learned about this from the frontier history of our country. It has shown clearly that when the lone western mountain men, the trappers, accepted integration into families and communities, and these further united into organized counties and states, and so on, they thereby gained, not lost, their true freedom—freedom conceived as the totality of opportunities *for* constructive endeavor, rather than as mere freedom *from* constraints. To be sure, the isolated mountain man had almost complete liberty, with almost no social restraints upon his mobility and behavior. He did not have to stay put or be a gentleman; he could do as he pleased, with virtually no custom or law to say yea or nay. But he was not *free* to achieve much of anything except to market his furs and satisfy a minimum of biological needs. When he married and became a settler, he had to give up most of his freedom *from,* but he thereby gained much more freedom *for*—for fuller biological and social existence, for creating family and community, for engaging in the arts and crafts, in commerce and politics, or in the building of systems of thought, all of which became possible only through communally integrated living. This is what organization, institutionalization, integration are for, and what they do accomplish when they function properly.

One is reminded here of what happens in nature, say, to water molecules when there is a change of state from water vapor to water liquid. In vapor they are very far apart and virtually free to move in any direction and with any speed, whereas in the liquid state they are very close together and much less mobile. They lose their complete freedom to move at random and become bound to one another, so that they can no longer move as freely as they did in the vapor. In the solid state, this binding is even more tight, so that there are definite structural interrelationships, as in snowflakes. In both cases, however, they acquire real freedom, i.e., a range of possibilities, to participate in the creation of many phenomena and realities that would have been completely beyond their capacity in their isolated state. Together they can contribute to the maintenance of the many important properties of liquids or solids, fluidity or rigidity, to the phenomena of boiling or melting, to the formation of the water drop or the snow crystal, to the transmission of sound or of light, and thus to the roar and sparkle of the waterfall, the rustle of the leaves or the irridescence of the butterfly wing, to the splashing sound of rain or the painting of the rainbow, which isolated molecules can't do. Molecules integrated into the structures of solids—for instance, metals—help to generate and transport electric power. In the nervous systems of men they participate in the transmission of decision-making messages by means of electric impulses. In plants they are involved in the production of mutations and thus in the emergence of new varieties and species. In an analogical sense the dignity and value of a molecule lies in its being a part of, not separate from, a process or communal endeavor where its freedom *from* is limited, but its freedom *for* is maximized.

Similarly, an individual person in a community, or in the overall new humanity, need not lose his identity or significance. It is much more likely that the more relationships he enters into there, the more unique a person he will be, and the more significant a function he will be able to perform therein. One of the serious problems right now is, and probably will be in the future, that many disadvantaged people do not have access to such participatory experience in the world. What they lack is not independence, but interaction, cooperative endeavor, interdependence. Here is a tremendous challenge. The solution we should seek is not to extricate the individual from the system, but to make him truly a part of it. The expected "new humanity" may indeed turn out to be a monstrous totalitarian dehumanizing machine. On the other hand, it may not. It is at least as probable that after it has passed through its initial transitional, experimental stage, it will be a genuinely democratic and humane societal organism in which its individual constituents can be truly themselves in the most meaningful way possible.

Newer Understandings of Reality and People

At this point there arises an extremely important question: What is a person? Before going into this, however, I should like us to consider what *anything* is, i.e., what the nature of reality is. For instance, what is a molecule, say the water molecule mentioned a while ago? It is a combination of two hydrogen atoms and one oxygen atom. But what is an atom of oxygen? The answer used to be quite obvious: an atom of oxygen is simply the smallest bit of a primordial substance called oxygen, just as a hydrogen atom is simply hydrogen. In the nineteenth century this answer seemed altogether self-evident—and quite sufficient. What more could be or needed to be said?

Now, however, such an answer seems quite inadequate, for we know that atoms are complex dynamic structures with many kinds of constituents, such as protons, neutrons, electrons, and many others. Also, in it occur many types of events. Scientists have come to speak of it, and define any particular species of atom, in terms of dynamic relationships and events, rather than substances. To ask what an atom is, or a proton, or an electron, is not to ask what it is made of, but how it interacts with other entities, and in what types of events it participates. An electron behaves in one way, and a proton in another—and *that* is the way we know it, and *that* is what it *is*. Its so-called properties do not derive from any supposed inherent essence alone, but from the presence of, and interaction with, other entities as well.

Moreover, such properties as temperature, hardness, fluidity, and friction are not the properties of individual molecules, or of other basic particles, but only of large swarms of them. They come into being by virtue of the interrelationships that appear when myriads of them aggregate to form matter in bulk. Until then they do not exist. So it has come about that what seems most real, and most basic, about things, and about reality in general, and what impresses itself upon our awareness most compellingly, is not *substance* in its insular uniqueness, but *relationship* noted or experienced in interactions and events.

Now, then, what is true of matter, is even more true of persons. A person is not what he is in and of himself, i.e., by virtue of his genetic inheritance only, but what he becomes and is in relationship to other beings, both persons and nonpersons. He *attains* his self and *has* a self by virtue of the way they affect him and he affects them. Men, like electrons and molecules, exist in fields of force and influence of many kinds. They are embedded in a vast network of dynamic relationships, happenings, and processes. And their human qualities depend on the continuous flux of those interrelations and interactions. If a newborn child were placed in a cell in virtually complete isolation, so that no interrelations with other entities could develop, and so no signals or information from outside could enter the cell and then the child's brain, the child could not develop into a person. It would become no more than a mass of protoplasm, perhaps a vegetable shaped like a human, but not a truly human being with a mind. Minds come into being not simply by birth (and perhaps not even at birth), but by virtue of the many experiences that are possible only in the presence of, and through interaction with, a dynamic environment.

This is why Clifford Geertz, anthropologist recently of the University of Chicago, has said:

There is no such thing as a human nature independent of culture. Men without culture would not be the clever savages of Golding's *Lord of the Flies* thrown back upon the cruel wisdom of their animal instincts; nor would they be the nature's noblemen of Enlightenment primitivism or even, as classical anthropological theory would imply, intrinsically talented apes who had somehow failed to find themselves. They would be unworkable monstrosities with very few useful instincts, fewer recognizable sentiments, and no intellect; mental basket cases. . . . Without men, no culture, certainly; but equally, and more significantly, without culture, no men.[6]

To this, John R. Platt, of the University of Michigan, adds: "Change the culture and you change the man."[7]

Extensive analysis of the implications of these newer insights reveals, however, not only that a thing or a person can be understood to exist and have meaning only in relation to, and in interaction with, other entities that are present to it; but that in an important sense a thing or person is at any instant the momentary state of the universe, since its field of influence is coextensive with the universe, and all of the universe thus participates in what it is as an event. The disintegration of an atomic fragment, the coming to rest of a heart, the cry of a baby, the brain participating in the birth of a poem, the mushrooming of a nuclear explosion, all these are universal in extent. Thus there is among us a growing sense of the cosmic relationship and involvement, and therefore of the cosmic consequentiality, of everything we do and are.

Human Values Defined by Relations

Therefore, for many men today, the new understanding of the relational and eventful character of reality has contributed greatly to the expansion and intensification of their sense of what is right or wrong, and morally responsible. Increasingly, they realize that relationship and interaction constitute the very ground of reality and meaning, and are therefore sacred, not to be tampered with irresponsibly. Likewise, wholeness, both personal and cosmic, has taken on new meaning as something absolutely fundamental to reality, both human and nonhuman. We now see that wholes are not only derivative, determined by their parts, but that the character and function of the parts depend upon the wholes. Surely the human heart, lungs, brain, and all other organs have this reciprocal and mutually determinative relationship to the whole of the human body.

All this leads, then, directly to the subject of values and moral standards, in terms of which the quality of men's decision-making toward the future is to be conceived and judged, and the character of the coming world is to be shaped. At this point I make an assumption, namely, that *man's values should be in harmony with the basic character of the universe, and that if they were, they would be in harmony with divine cosmic purposes.* If this be granted, it would seem to follow that those values are legitimate and consistent with the cosmic scheme of things which tend to support and maximize optimum mutuality, relationship, interdependence, and wholeness; and that those are undesirable and cosmically incongruous which tend toward the maximum of utter independence, self-sufficiency, isolation, and fragmentation. That is wrong which makes for the enhancement or glorification of the *individual unto himself,* rather than of the *individual in community.* Herein lies the potential for a tremendous clash in the realm of values. Which shall prevail, the values based on the supremacy of independence or those arising out of interdependence? Abstract general statements such as these have, of course, little meaning practically, until they are interpreted and illustrated by specifics; and I shall presently want to talk briefly about those.

Reality Evolves, So Human Values Must

Before doing this, however, I want to call attention to one more of the fundamental, constitutive characteristics of reality that provides, I feel, a criterion for the acceptability of values. Reality is historical and developmental, rather than merely inert and fixed; and it is creative and productive, rather than sterile and only conservative; and it is open, rather than closed, to new possibilities and thrusts toward the future. Reality seems not to have come into being full-blown, but gradually, and over a long period of time. In the nineteenth century there came to us the insight that the biological, geological, and probably astronomical features of the universe evolved by a developmental process. It remained for the twentieth century, however, to discover that matter itself, the very atoms once thought to be eternal and unchangeable, has also evolved. We have gotten used to the idea that long ago there were no men on earth, and earlier still, no animals, and before that no plants and no life whatsoever—at least in our part of the universe. Now, it seems, we shall have to get used to the idea that once upon a time there was no water, no land, no rocks, no snowflakes or any other kind of crystals; and, alas, no molecules, and no atoms, but only the so-called elementary particles (the constituents of atoms), or at most only the very simple hydrogen atoms. Then the development began, yielding by what we may call "aggregation" the many kinds of atoms, and then the very many kinds of molecules, including the very large ones that replicate themselves, and thus exhibit the most primitive form of life. Then there developed, in the inorganic realm, the large aggregations, namely, the rocks, mountains, and planets, and then the whole gamut of vast astronomical systems.

It must be said, then, that matter, and probably all other reality, is basically developmental, productive, and creative, bringing forth under novelty from time to time. And there has been an unmistakable trend or direction in this development: from the simple to the complex, from the small to the large, from the isolated individual entities to combinations and integrated systems, and to community. In the light of this, it seems not unreasonable to expect that the next great emergence or development in the further evolution of the world may well be the cultural aggregation of the many individual men into one integrated mankind. In any case, it seems clear that if our values are to be in harmony with long-range cosmic trends—and divine intent—they must be such as not to hinder or inhibit development and change, and the emergence of the utterly novel, but to facilitate them, and thus to contribute to the building of a mankind and world characterized at its ground by development—as well as the relational qualities we have been considering. Another way of saying this is that our values must be future-oriented.

Now then, which of our traditional values are threatened by this prospect? Some not at all, as I see it—for instance, those derived from Biblical faith. Among these are what Paul called the "fruit of the Spirit": "love, joy, peace, patience, kindness, goodness, faithfulness, gentleness, self-control"; also such others as confidence, courage, belief, truth, beauty, honesty, love of God, love of neighbor. Surely none of these clash with the values we have identified as basic to reality itself and as fundamental to the future. Indeed it would seem that in principle the former are identical with the latter.

On the other hand, many other traditional values will certainly be challenged, for instance: all those which are tantamount to the demand for complete independence, for either the individual or the community separately; and those valued simply "for their own sake" (such as knowledge or beauty for its own sake) or for oneself only; or those taken as unchangeable absolutes (in the traditional sense), such as the absolutes of ethical theory and moral practice, or those of political, economic, or religious belief.

Among the values I would list as indispensable in the tomorrows are those envisioning a proper balance between individual and communal rights, such as adequate living space, size of families, purity of the human genetic stream, new patterns of work and play, together with new ways of supporting endeavors that are not usually regarded as "work for profit." I cite these few only as typical of many others. Not least among these are the ones arising from the new mutuality and interdependence relationship that man must achieve with nature regarded as an ecosystem, in which he is himself deeply embedded, for instance: the value of a proper ecological balance in nature, the value of wilderness, the rights of nature and its denizens not to be exploited irresponsibly. The crucial point here is that the new world must be a community not only of people but of all beings—human and nonhuman—that together make up the whole of the world and are interdependent upon one another. And this calls for values of truly universal brotherhood such as were articulated long ago by Francis, and are being reconceived so sensitively today, in terms of evolutionary kinship, by Loren Eiseley.

Threats to and Resources for Achieving New Values

So far I have argued that the new world we have envisioned *should* and *can* be built by man—with God. There is nothing that makes this impossible in principle. The question that remains is whether man *will* build it, and whether technology is likely to be on the whole a constructive or destructive force in this undertaking. As you may have suspected all along, I am one of those who believe (though they do not *know*) that such a new world *will* come into being, and that it will happen in the finite future, and that significant steps in that direction will be taken in the twenty-first century. This is, of course, not inevitable. The extent and power of evil in the world is vast. Even more vast, however, is the power of goodness, and of the creative and redemptive (remedial) presence of God in it. With Paul I believe that "the suffering we now endure bears no comparison with the splendor" of the future, and that the present groaning of "the whole universe in all its parts" is as though it were "in the pangs of childbirth." Yes, the world *is* in travail; but it is the travail of giving birth—

to a new and splendid world. And it is my conviction that, much popular opinion to the contrary, the nature of technology is *not* such as to abort this birth. Despite its many obvious human weaknesses, it is a remarkable instrumentality for good, and for creative change, and as such one of the great and potent gifts of God to man. Without it the creating of the new world would not be possible.

Technology provides means for creating new materials, relationships, and processes. It provides means by which true global interdependence and mutuality can become a reality. The worldwide communications network it has produced makes possible virtually instantaneous global participation in public human experience. Together with science it is the most powerful influence for international understanding, cooperation, and unification that exists now among us. Also, I suggest, it provides powerful tools for remedial action against misfortune and evil among men, and for transforming them for good. What comes to mind here is the great array of new techniques dealing curatively and transformatively with the maladjusted and mentally ill, by means of drugs, surgery, chemical and electric shock treatment, psychological and psychiatric treatment, and possibly prenatal genetic management.

Isn't there grave danger, however, that the immense power conferred by science and technology will fall into the hands of evil and power-hungry men? Yes, there is; and, of course, we have had Hitlers and Stalins in our time. But, for faith, danger is not something to be sidestepped or avoided. Instead of being stopped by danger, faith faces and goes out to meet and challenge it. Let us not forget that while men have always feared the new, especially new power and new ideas that make for power, in the long run the minuses and the plusses of the new have in the past added up to a positive, beneficent result.

My plea is that by all means we look at all the possibilities of the technological future very critically, but not as though dominated by fear. Tremendous good may come out of it if we proceed courageously and critically—and responsibly. Technology is not of itself either humanizing or dehumanizing. It is whatever we make of it. Its basic purpose and nature are benevolent. Its predominant motivations have always been to be useful to mankind. Thus far its impact on man's cultural evolution has been on the whole genuinely humanizing. It has given men new freedoms and new possibilities for more abundant life. Whether man will use these possibilities to the best advantage remains to be seen. This much is sure, however, that if he does not, it will not be because he is not utterly free and able to do so.

This, then, leads me to my last point. For me, the term "science" refers not only to the natural sciences but to the social sciences as well. Likewise, I take "technology" to include social technology. I emphasize this because I feel that the most difficult problems facing us will be those for which we shall need the help especially of social technology, namely, those involved in reshaping men's values to conform to the needs of the future, and in getting this done "on time."

There is among us a pronounced sense of urgency about this. We realize that time has become an exceedingly important factor in the situation, and that we may not have enough of it before being overwhelmed catastrophically by the pressures of excessive population and pollution, and that any new ways of life we may be able to devise may come too late, that is, after the truly human quality of our existence has vanished, or we have disappeared in a holocaust of nuclear explosion. I suggest, however, that the physical problems can be solved with relative ease before then, though, of course, at a tremendous price. What will be most difficult is getting ourselves and all mankind to see, think, value, and make decisions in a new mode, and to develop new points of view, new customs and standards of behavior, that are consonant with the character of the new world we want to build.

The sad fact is that with all their vaunted prowess in hard-sell persuasion, the social technologies—among which I count education, counseling, labor and management negotiation, lawmaking and enforcement, politics, diplomacy, and so on—know as yet far too little about how the human mind works, and how desirable outcomes in thought, human relations, and life-styles can be brought about noncoercively. Here is where technology as a whole is weakest as an agent of man and God for the creation of a new culture and the new man. Nevertheless, there is here, I feel, a huge potential for good, which we must make the most of and count on as a major resource for the future. And it is here that religion faces its supreme challenge vis-à-vis technology. What can it contribute in this situation *positively and creatively,* aside from simply issuing warnings and protests, important and indispensable as these are?

Biblical (Hebraic-Christian) religion is, I feel, in an especially strong position to make positive and creative contributions—because of its long tradition of this-worldliness, its earthiness that places high value upon the concrete in life, its orientation and thrust toward the future, and its emphases on personal and social service. Its ecclesiastical and lay leadership should therefore put itself on record as wishing to be allied with, rather than opposed to, the forces of technology as these devote themselves to the improvement of the common lot of mankind, and to the ushering in of the new world.

I believe in man and in God, and in a splendid future that will surely come if man labors *with* God. I cannot see a splendid future achieved without him, that is, by man going his own independent way, as though he were himself God.

NOTES

1. Leslie Dewart, *The Future of Belief* (Herder & Herder, Inc., 1966), p. 193.

2. Marshall McLuhan, *Understanding Media: The Extensions of Man* (McGraw-Hill Book Company, Inc., 1964), pp. 3 ff.

3. *Ibid.,* p. vii.

4. Karl Jaspers, *The Origin and Goal of History* (London: Routledge & Kegan Paul, Ltd., 1953), pp. 126, 127, 139, 193.

5. *Ibid.,* p. 117.

6. John R. Platt (ed.), *New Views of the Nature of Man* (The University of Chicago Press, 1965); see Ch. 5: Clifford Geertz, "The Impact of the Concept of Culture in the Concept of Man," p. 112.

7. John R. Platt, *The Step to Man* (John Wiley & Sons, Inc., 1966), p. 159.

CHAPTER IV

Biblical Symbols
in a Scientific Culture

Langdon Gilkey

Our theme concerns the meaning and use of Biblical symbols in a scientific culture. In getting at this subject, we must first understand clearly that such uses are a *problem* for a scientific culture, and why this is so. Biblical symbols, like all religious symbols, are multivalent in form. That is, on the one hand, they seem to speak about concrete historical events (a first creation, the exodus, Jesus of Nazareth, the new work of God in the future, and so on) and thus to tell simple *stories* of the past and make predictions about the future. On the other hand, they point beyond these events in space-time to an actor or reality in them who transcends the phenomenal world, who is more than a creature, a man, a secondary cause, a finite thing among other things—namely, to God, the Creator and Ruler of all things. Thus they refer at one and the same time both to matters of fact and to what transcends matters of fact, and this is the essential character of religious language. The queer traits of this language arise here as well as its power and necessity—and, above all, its difficulties in a scientific world.

The difficulties stem from the character of a scientific culture itself. For such a culture, at least in its modern forms, all that is real, and therefore all that can be intelligibly talked about, are the finite, natural, and historical factors visible on the surface of the natural and historical worlds. A transcendent, ultimate, sacred dimension or factor is thus unreal to us; we don't know what it might be like or what talk about it means—and we certainly feel at a loss to establish or prove anything anyone might say about it. Thus religious symbols, pointing to the transcendent in the finite, the mystery beyond the observable and calculable relations between things and persons—whether in nature or in history—seem to us either prescientific and superstitious, offering us wrong explanations about finite relations, or of psychological importance only, expressing our own anxious, churning insides, their repressed hatreds and wishes. For these reasons, both metaphysics and theology have been ghostlike in our time, for their referents: "reality," "actuality," or "God," have seemed, like shades in the light of day, to have whimpered and vanished from our midst.

Every form of recent theology has sought to deal with these difficulties. Some, as did much of liberalism, have sought to "join up," to regard religious truths as the results of conclusions of scientific inquiry—as when evolution was flattered by the name of God (or vice versa). Or with the Kantians and the neo-orthodox, they have tried to separate the two realms rigorously, finding religious truths relevant only to moral or existential matters, and not to scientific inquiries at all. To me—and I think recent theological history bears this out—neither road has led anywhere. Science in the long run disavows—or better, devours—the religious conclusions based on its own inquiries, and no form of religious truth can remain permanently separated from what science knows. As the shaky status currently of metaphysics indicates, any form of truth transcendent to scientific truth finds life precarious at best in modernity. Whether one is a poor theologian apparently frightened by demons and angels or a bewildered metaphysician bewitched by language, it matters little: neither one seems to say anything in a scientific culture except about his own confusions. So our question remains: Where *do* religious and so Biblical symbols fit in a scientific culture? Are they, like magical incantations, something that has permanently gone—or, if not yet that, something that we should, if we be modern men, be permanently done with?

So it appears. But the moment one looks more carefully at our culture, especially its scientific and technical aspects, this diagnosis and prescription suddenly seems premature. For it is evident that unfortunately our cultural life confronts many of the same baffling issues as did other ages; that with all its knowledge and its know-how, it experiences much of the same ambiguity; that it knows deeply all the same searing fears and anxieties; and that it looks desperately for grounds for the same sort of hopes. Our culture too knows the demons of fate, sin, and death, and we too seek to comprehend them with our own forms of religious and mythical symbolism. When we look scientifically into these matters, such transcendent dimensions seem to vanish away—but this is an optical illusion of a scientific culture. They don't vanish at all. They return full-blown, a whole pantheon of religious and mythical figures—dressed, to be sure, in white coats and not in long feathers—to calm our fears and answer our querulous doubts. Even the most secular of cultures can never succeed in disinfecting our world of religion: for the man who does the disinfecting merely takes it all on himself and becomes, in his own eyes and that of his culture, only the greatest shaman of them all!

Where is it, then, that religious symbols, albeit confused, incoherent, and unempirical, appear in our cultural life, radically secular as it believes itself to be? Do we think religiously about our origins? Do we find heaven populated with gods and demons, or long for an eternity beyond the wheel of time? The answer is, of course, no. These have been the religious symbols of other cultures, and naturally, like all else in a cultural whole, the religious symbols of modernity take forms different from them. Origins are not sacred to us; the question of our beginnings fascinates us, but there is no sacral or exemplar significance to us about our primitive forebears. Generally, then, questions about origins are for modernity "problems" for the special sciences, for astronomy, physics, chemistry and biochemistry, biology, genetics, physical anthropology, and archaeology. Correspondingly, eternity has no allure to us; all that is real for us is in time, and so the sacred does not transcend passage. If, then, religious myths and symbols do not point either to beginnings or to eternity, where do they point? Is not the secular view after all correct, that such forms of language have vanished for us in all but the name? Let us try another hypothesis: important religious symbols "fit" a culture, and thus modern religious symbolism will be modern in its shape. So in analyzing the characteristically strong points about modernity, we may find where its important religious symbols gain their meaning and usage—and then see how these compare with our traditional Biblical symbols.

Salvatory Myths from Science

Characteristically, modern man lives in developing time and looks forward into the future for his sense of fulfillment. He does not find his identity by repeating an eternal structure established by the gods, or ingrained in natural harmonies; rather, his identity comes through the realization of his own freedom, in re-creating and refashioning what is given to him, in making out of the past a new structure more valuable than the old. If modern man believes anything—and he does—it is that meaning is created by the passage of process into the future, and that this meaning is in part, if not as a whole, the result of his own decisions, his own intelligence, and his own moral intentions. The creativity of passage, the wonder of human autonomy, the increment of value and meaning in the future—these are the characteristic faiths of a secular culture. Strangely, two factors have been prominent in creating this ethos, on the one hand, the Biblical view of time and history, and on the other, science; and thus in this general sense our modern religious myths can be called "scientific."

Our modern religious symbol systems, not unsurprisingly, express in variant forms this modern faith. There have been two great "cosmic" or global faiths of modernity: the liberal belief in Progress or in Evolution as a cosmic law of development, and Marxism; each represents variations of this basic theme. Although both claim to be "science" and are looked on as science by their adherents—for a scientific culture, all truth and so all religious truth must be "scientific"—actually, both transcend science into religious mythology.[1] Both make assertions about process as a whole, and so their language is essentially multivalent, referring to the ultimate structure of things and not just to matters of fact.

Thus have they been expanded beyond the limits of the original scientific discipline (biology and economics, respectively), and as a consequence neither one is verifiable or falsifiable by any empirical tests. The truth of these myths functions as does religious truth, not by demonstrations but by the way it answers our existential questions about the nature of process as a whole and our place within it. Consequently, these are adhered to by faith rather than by inquiry, by a spiritual existence in and commitment to a community that lives by these symbolic systems.

Secondly, their meaning is that of myth and not that of science; for they function as myths in our cultural life, each providing a framework of ultimacy within which both public history and private destiny make sense. And each has provided fundamental norms and standards for communal life, for political, ethical, educational, and even cognitive judgments. No system of scientific ideas functions in this way. Thus a scientific culture finds at its base a symbol system that itself claims to be science, and yet which performs for that culture all that a system of religious symbols once did, and so whose meaning and validity are those characteristic of other religious systems.

As the history of these two illustrates, moreover, global myths in a scientific or secular culture, even those which the culture itself has developed, have a hard time and so a short life. Since they too are multivalent, pointing to an ultimate order or pattern in visible things, they are subject to the same criticism as were older religious systems. And the fact that each one paraded as science made it all the worse. Both cosmic Evolution and the Material Dialectic of history have been tested by the empirical facts in biology and history, and thus reduced to the level of scientific hypotheses instead of that of global myths. As a consequence, in the twentieth century, evolution has tended to be reduced from the cosmic principle it surely was at the end of the nineteenth century to a respected but limited—and so no longer existential—theory in biology. And when it reappears in global form—as in Teilhard de Chardin—most scientists are quick to assure us that this is mystical philosophy at best and not biology. In any case, evolution no longer dominates as it once did historical, sociological, political, ethical, and religious studies, giving to them their fundamental horizon of self-interpretation. Much the same has been occurring, I gather, among at least the European representatives of the Marxist faith.

The twentieth century, we suggest, has tended to devour the religious mythology that its parent, the nineteenth century, produced. Nevertheless, while global or cosmic myths are not to our taste—science tends to mistrust unverified statements about its legitimate object, the universe—we do still have our myths. For if a scientific culture finds it hard to believe in an ultimate order of change and destiny—if for it, God and the gods are in this sense dead—still one thing it does believe in is science itself, in the illuminating and healing power of inquiry. The world may to us be utterly disenchanted—to use Peter Gay's phrase[2]—but we are by no means disenchanted with the critical intelligence that has stripped it of its sacrality. And thus a new form of the Gnostic myth has appeared in the twentieth century: man may be on his own in a blind, purposeless, undirected cosmos; but now that he knows how to know, and is thus free to do whatever he will with his world and himself, he can at last, like some Indra or Zeus of old, take control of the material flux that has produced him, and directing both his biological and his cultural evolution, master his own destiny. Let us listen to several major voices in contemporary science expressing this myth: respectively George Gaylord Simpson, Theodosius Dobzhansky, Victor Ferkiss, and Immanuel Mesthene.

From Simpson:

Man has risen, not fallen. He can choose to develop his capacities as the highest animal and to try to rise still farther, or he can choose otherwise. The choice is his responsibility, and his alone. There is no automatism that will carry him upward without choice or effort, and there is no trend solely in the right direction. Evolution has no purpose; man must apply this for himself . . . the old evolution was and is essentially amoral. The new evolution involves knowledge, including the knowledge of good and evil. The most essential material factor in the new evolution seems to be this: knowledge, together, necessarily, with its spread and inheritance.[3]

From Dobzhansky:

Man is not only evolved, he is evolving. This is a source of hope in the abyss of despair. . . . Man and man alone knows that the world evolves and that he evolves with it. By changing what he knows about the world man changes the world that he knows: and by changing the world in which he lives man changes himself. Changes may be deteriorations or improvement; the hope lies in the possibility that changes resulting from knowledge may also be directed by knowledge. Evolution needs no longer be a destiny imposed from without; it may be conceivably controlled by man, in accordance with his wisdom and his values.[4]

From Ferkiss:

The logical climax of evolution can be said to have occurred when, as is now imminent, a sentient species deliberately and directly assumes control of its own evolution. . . . If man can do or be whatever he wishes, how shall he choose? What should be his criteria of choice? In the past, nature and ignorance set limits to man's freedom and his follies, now they need no longer stand in his way, and technological man will be free even to destroy the possibility of freedom itself.[5]

And from Mesthene:

We have now, or know how to acquire, the technical capability to do very nearly anything we want. Can we transplant human hearts, control personality, order the weather that suits us, travel to Mars or Venus? Of course we can, if not now or in five or ten years, then certainly in twenty-five or in fifty or a hundred.[6]

We are dealing here with an example of fundamental symbolic thinking, thinking that is mythical and religious in form. Scientific Man as knower and manipulator of his environment and himself is here pictured as his own savior, as able through his knowledge, the freedom it gives him, and his resultant decisions, to shape what was once a *blind* process of change (cosmic evolution) into a *purposive* process of change (cultural evolution) in which human values can now be more fully realized. The fates *over* man can by gnosis become forces used *for* man. As we shall show, in its own relevant area, history, this myth is totally unempirical; like all myths, it deals with the mystery of our selfhood, our freedom and intelligence in relation to the forces that determine us; and, as do religions generally, it answers our anxious questions about our destiny; it expresses the bases of our most fundamental confidence and hopes. It seems nonetheless quite commonsensical to us, obvious in fact, and it is, as we have just seen, expressed unquestionably by our intellectual leaders—much as fundamental Christian beliefs used to be uttered by the intellectual leaders of the past. And no wonder; it is the common religion of our sophisticated, scientific culture. To challenge it evokes real resentment, and, as a professor of biology in California said once to me when I asked him why on earth he believed that in the future man could or would thusly resolve his basic problems—he answered, "Well, you have to believe *something,* don't you?"

Let us examine this anthropocentric myth with some care. We shall, I think, find that even though it is dominant among most of the intelligent men, the scientists in our culture, that it has several very serious flaws. As a form of religious belief or confidence, it is not very impressive; for it is in fact self-contradictory, nonempirical, against all the relevant evidence, and socially and politically dangerous. Let us note, our critique is *not* directed at science but at the religious mythology, the sacral aura, science has produced. It is when it poses as our savior, as religious, that science becomes problematic or idolatrous, as when religion posed as an omnicompetent informant on all issues. In the process of this criticism we shall see more clearly by contrast the use of the corresponding Biblical symbols about man and his destiny.

The Paradox of Scientific Myths

First of all, this myth about scientific man as his own savior is self-contradictory. This should not be a surprise to us, since the myth deals with an old puzzle, namely, the relation of destiny and freedom, of determinism and free will—though those who utter it would be surprised to hear this—and paradoxes in philosophy and theology on *that* issue are, of course, legion. However, because it is simplistic and scientific in its form, this myth pushes the paradox into self-contradiction. What do we mean?

The myth concerns, as the quotations indicated, man's power through critical inquiry, scientific conclusions, and a sensible moral use of his knowledge to create a new environment outside him and a new nature for himself, and thus to control by his own intelligence and moral will the forces outside and inside man that heretofore have determined him. What were blind, purposeless, determining fates over man can now through scientific knowledge of these determining forces be turned into forces to be used purposefully by man to establish a more humanly meaningful existence.

Here the contradiction begins to appear. Scientific knowledge is necessarily of determining forces, that which is nonintentional, and necessary, and so that which can be manipulated, measured, calculated, and tested. Thus as a method of inquiry, science abstracts from and so cannot find intentionality or freedom anywhere in its objects; it can only discover the determining, nonintentional factors in things. As Julian Steward, the cultural anthropologist, has said: "Any assumption that teleological or orthogenetic principles, Divine interventions or free will are at work would nullify scientific explanation . . . science must proceed *as if* natural laws operate consistently and without exception, as if all cultures and all aspects of human behavior had determinants."[7] The knowledge of man that science produces is thus of man as a determined being; it presupposes for its own coherence and meaning that man is such a being, and insofar as it promises control over man, his nature and destiny, it must presuppose that man is through and through a necessitated being. Otherwise, this knowledge must be regarded as essentially abstractive, partial, and incomplete, and then the image of control of man through science contains no promise of the kind of control over himself and his destiny that is here offered to us. Insofar as men are free, and can "look back" at their investigator, cheat on a scientific test, or otherwise bring forth creative surprises the investigator had not predicted, in just that far knowledge of man as determined is intrinsically incomplete and the control over man correspondingly incomplete. The intelligibility of the promised salvation depends on man as a determined being, determined totally by forces that can be understood, mastered, and manipulated by scientific knowledge.

On the other hand, the same image proclaims precisely the opposite picture of man. For it presupposes that scientific man, insofar as he knows these determining forces that control things, has the freedom to use that knowledge creatively to control those forces for his own purposes. And thus, although it contradicts what they have just said, men such as Steward—not to mention Simpson and Dobzhansky—in speaking of the *uses* of scientific knowledge, as opposed to its conclusions, talk freely of "choices," "decisions," "moral aims and purposes," i.e., all that was *ever* meant and more by free will. Here, man is seen as the free manipulator of all the determining forces around him, standing above and outside of those forces, surveying them and so directing them purposefully, a direct contradiction to its own presupposition, namely, that man is determined. When we proclaim the possibility that man can now determine his own destiny by controlling the forces outside and inside him, human freedom and intentionality are given a more unlimited range than in any other religious vision that I know of—man is here not at all a mite on a sea of determination, but a mighty ruler over that sea. Surely a myth that promises man's intentional and moral control over the forces of destiny because man now knows the forces that totally determine his life is blatantly contradictory, and makes similar theological paradoxes look mild indeed! The confused phrase "cultural evolution" implies both sides of this contradiction: the determining forces of evolutionary development, and the intentional control of man over his own cultural life. "Cultural evolution" in implying both sides of this unmediated contradiction in fact implies nothing—except the hubris of the anthropologist that at last he has uncovered the forces that make history tick!

We can, I think, understand this contradiction by recalling that science has two roles in our cultural life, which point our thought about man in two quite opposite directions. First, science appears as a body of conclusions about man, hypotheses about the determining factors in man's nature, biological, genetic, psychological, social, and so on. Here man appears as a small determined object in the flux of vast impersonal forces studied by science; and here no hint of free will appears or can appear. When we ask therefore what science *knows* about man, the answer adds up to the picture of a determined creature pushed necessarily by unintentional forces outside and inside him, a mite on a vast natural sea.

Science, however, also appears, not as a body of conclusions, but as a vastly creative activity of human intelligence, in which activity autonomous man manipulates his environment, experiences his own rational consciousness, is aware of himself as dedicated to and determined by freely chosen ideals and convictions, and looks forward through that knowledge to his own control over the forces he has studied. As a human activity, experienced by the scientist in himself and in his community, science produces in men and has produced in modern culture as a whole one of the most vivid experiences of intentional human freedom, of creative autonomy, that history has ever produced—as these extravagant words about man's control over destiny, being lord of his own fate, clearly indicate. This is, let us note, a different mode of cognition than is the other. It is not man as an object that is known, but here scientific man as a subject is aware of himself, of his intentional freedom, his rational consciousness and his own moral purposes—which, of course, is how all categories of free will and of "spirit" have arisen in past philosophy and theology! The difficulty is that these two quite different aspects of man, gained by different modes of cognition, both of which have been affirmed unequivocally by the voice of science, are not here mediated or brought to any kind of coherence. How could they be unless another level of knowing and speaking is seen as a possibility, a philosophical or theological level? For such a mediation or bringing to coherence of these two aspects of experience requires that science recognize that its *conclusions* about man are partial and incomplete; that man's self-understanding must be based on another level of self-awareness; and that finally science must turn to philosophy or theology if it is to understand *itself* as a human activity. If, however, one deliberately confines important speaking to scientific talk about man, then both of these aspects are felt and therefore asserted—But a contradiction results—for man as investigated by science is *known* as determined, and man as investigator is *felt* as free—a contradiction that can be both silly and dangerous when we say, "Science knows nothing of man as a personal subject, and therefore we can legitimately control man for our own purposes!"

Need for Biblical Symbols of Man's Worth

The myth, therefore, taken "straight" could be dangerous as well as contradictory. It is generally not dangerous because it is in fact *not* taken straight by men who are liberals, that is, when it is qualified by other symbols deeply influential in our cultural life, especially Biblical symbols about the value of man as a personal, inward, individual being.

The model here with which we think out our hopes for the future is a picture of man as the knower controlling other things through his knowledge in order to enact on them his moral purposes. The source of the model is clearly man's successful technological control over nature. Here science and its resulting technology have made it possible for us to control our environment for many genuinely creative and important purposes, producing food, securing water and heat, eliminating wastage, getting us from one place to another, and so on, and finally sustaining our bodies through the application of medical knowledge. The ambiguity of this whole effort we shall discuss in a moment. Meanwhile, until only yesterday, this seemed to us unalloyed in its creativity; almost nothing but good had come for man out of his conquest through knowledge of the natural world that surrounded him—or such was our dream.

However, we should realize that with all its now evident ambiguity, man's control over nature is a different thing from man's control over *man,* and that the latter raises ethical problems for the future that technology heretofore has not even raised. For if the knower is to enact his knowledge on men, he must use and apply the determining forces he has discovered, and through them determine "for his own purposes" the life, the possibilities, and the actuality of the other man. Scientific man controls Man only by controlling men—and in social matters such control inevitably has implications of political tyranny and the dehumanization of man that are horrendous to contemplate. A strictly scientific view of man, taken seriously, might tend to regard society as a vast laboratory in which only the scientist and his political bosses retain their freedom. A good many people in our culture feel more comfortable when our fundamental problems are made "objective," that is, made into problems for objective analysis and external control. But to see social issues as *objectified* problems to be resolved by expert control means something else *politically*—namely, the control of other men as if *they* were objectified, made into objects.

The sciences of man can in truth bring great benefit to the human venture, let us be clear about that. But they can only do so if the scientific elite is willing to grant to men as the object of their knowledge and control the same freedom and personal identity that they presuppose themselves to have as the purposive knowers or subjects who effect that control. A sense of the mystery and inviolability of the person, both in his personal and his political relations—that he is made in the image of God and so cannot be made an object of my purposes—however noble they seem to me —is necessary if we are to understand at all what scientific knowledge might mean creatively for the future. A scientific culture can become demonic if science is not used by men whose self-understanding, and so whose public actions, are guided by symbols that transcend the limits of scientific inquiry and so illumine and express the spiritual, personal, and free dimensions of man's being.

Such, then, is the first ethical use of Biblical symbols. Not that they tell us what to do, but that they provide the framework of comprehension within which we may see dimly what is right to do. If we know deeply that men, even other men, are also made in the image of God, are free, self-determining, personal, and so valuable beings, then our actions on the basis of our knowledge will be tempered by this understanding; and we will realize how important it is—when we embark on prospects of controlling man's life and destiny—to preserve man's freedom and self-determination in the process. This is not to say that this image of man as personal is useful but untrue. The sciences are also aware of this dimension of freedom and intentionality—but generally only in themselves as knowers and doers. We must have a deeper symbolism that expresses our knowledge and certainty that this is a universal characteristic of man as object as well as subject of knowledge and control.

Value of Biblical Symbols of Sin and Grace

Another significant use of religious symbolism and so of theological reflection in a scientific culture concerns not so much the question of the preservation of the personal dignity of the object of control as it does the problem of the freedom and the wisdom of the controller himself. Theology can well point out that there is a good deal *less* freedom in the scientific knower and controller through his knowledge than most descriptions of the potential uses of science in the future seem to assume. It is strange but true that in this context theology stresses the determination of man, while the mythology of scientific modernity emphasizes his absolute and unconditioned freedom. Our suggestion, in other words, is that some of that sense of determination of man's reason and will by forces outside and within himself, which determination is taken for granted in scientific accounts of man as an object, should be read back into their thoughts about themselves as scientific men as subjects, as knowers and doers—when modern scientific culture utters its myth of controlling our destiny, of bending even evolution to human purposes!

Knowledge is power. It results almost invariably in the power to control that which is now known. Knowledge about man can, therefore, lead to the power to control other men, and it is through that new potentiality for control that our knowledge appears to be able to direct human destiny itself. But new power, even power through knowledge, by no means guarantees the virtue or the wisdom of the man with power, the controller, the self-control of the man who now wields the power. When men, even scientific men, exert social power over other men, they have left far behind the innocence of the laboratory, the engineering camp, and the hospital; now they have entered the murky and ambiguous realm of politics. And with regard to the uses of power in society and so in political life, the only valid experimental evidence about how men use power is given us by the study of history—not by the benign experiences of the scientist in his own laboratory. History is, unfortunately, grimly unequivocal on one point, namely, that power universally corrupts the users of power. The men who control others in the political arena are not as free to control themselves through reason and moral will as are those in the laboratory, or as they themselves assume because of their good intentions. With regard to political and social matters, men are in fact determined by forces of ambition, of self-interest, and of anxiety about their class, nation, or race—forces which twist the rationality of their minds and the morality of their wills, and so which seriously diminish their control over what they do. The machinations of the physician's union with regard to the public uses of medical knowledge illustrate this change from the integrity of the office and the laboratory to the unreasoned, prejudiced, and fanatic atmosphere of the political arena.

Somehow in history rational plans and good intentions seldom achieve full realization. Unlike corresponding plans in the laboratory or at the space center, they become ethically muddied in their enactment, and create unintended evils as often as intended good. Almost inevitably, whether we be idealistic revolutionaries or moral defenders of freedom, in history we move from the innocence of moral intention to the corruption of actualization. Consider, for example, the vast difference in the success of its outcome between the war on the moon and the war on poverty; or consider how a host of noble revolutionaries such as Sukarno, Mao, Nkrumah of Ghana, Castro, to name only contemporary examples, have been corrupted tyrants in a few years' time; and saddest of all, how our own involvement with possibly the best of moral intentions in Viet-Nam, has ended in an evil morass of death, fear, guilt, and cruelty. Each illustrates the loss of control over what we are doing and over its moral consequences, a loss that seems endlessly to repeat itself. In history, men appear to have little control over what they do, for they cannot fully determine the ultimate direction and integrity of their own wills, much less the course of the history in which they are immersed. The great increase in man's ability to control what is outside of him through technology has not led to any corresponding increase either in man's control over himself or over his fate. Rather, it is still true that in the political arena, an increment of power—of freedom in that sense—ironically tends to increase man's bondage to his own self-concern, and thus to raise rather than to lower the level of what was *unintended* in the fated destiny that he bequeaths to his own children.

Scientists often say, "It is not a problem for science if men use our products irrationally, if our political and moral life has not 'kept pace' with our science and technology. Clearly the fault lies in these other spheres of our culture—the moral, political, and religious spheres—for which *we* are not responsible." This is to beg the question by means of a myth. For political and social history *is* irrational. Man has been and is irrational in history—all the evidence cries out this truth: man has little self-control, and therefore little rational control over the course of historical events. This is the political situation—to believe the opposite, or that because of science all this will change, is sheer myth, better called a credulous faith in Eden than by any other name. If, therefore, we think rationally and so empirically about science and its uses, let us not think of science as it might have appeared in Eden, but on the contrary in relation to *actuality,* to our often irrational, frequently chaotic, and on occasion, tragic history.

This is perhaps the most important wisdom that theology might bring to a scientific culture. Just as man as a child of God is more free and personal than scientific knowledge declares him to be, so even scientific and technological men, as sinners among sinners, are more determined—by the social forces of class, nation, and race, and by the inward forces of greed, ambition, hostility, and anxiety for themselves and their group—than those who propose social uses and who cheer the benign prospects of our knowledge seem to assume.

Only if a scientific society recognizes through some form of symbolization these two aspects of the mystery of man—his value and yet his evident lack of virtue—and so only if it realizes the ambiguity with which its new knowledge and potent techniques will be used, can it with creativity deal with the ecological, social, political, and moral problems which these new powers are now raising. For if man still has great difficulty in controlling himself, even when he means well, then surely we must be much wiser and more careful when we embark socially on programs designed to control our destiny and so ourselves through scientific knowledge. The myth, in other words, of man "come of age," and so as now free and virtuous man through an increase in his knowledge, is not only a self-contradictory and empirically inaccurate myth. Even more, it can be a dangerous myth in applied science. For if man believes this about himself, and heaven help us if he does, then he will charge ahead to control and remake himself and the world, justifying himself all the while by his own good intentions, and yet actually, because he knows not what he does, controlling others for his own ends—establishing, for example, through *American* technological dominance the "American type" as the goal of man's new evolutionary destiny. On the basis of the validity of its realistic symbols about man, therefore, Christian theology can utter a most helpful warning with regard to the continuing need for rational social control over the learned controllers.

A scientific age, which has added immensely to our understanding and so to our powers, has not made us more virtuous, nor has it made the meanings of our life any more secure. Our control over ourselves and our consequent control over our own destiny seems in no wise to be more within our grasp than before. The old theological problems of the use man makes of his freedom, of his bondage to self-interest, and of the ultimate meaning of the human story have been dissolved neither by the physical nor by the life sciences. Rather, they have been precisely increased by them.

As is well known, Greek philosophy, like modern mythology, tended to identify knowing with virtue, our ability to know with our ability to solve significant problems and dilemmas. Though this Hellenic identification is also questionable (for example, see Paul's remarks on it in Rom., ch. 7), nevertheless it should be noted that Greek thought presents a better case than does the modern version of the Gnostic hope. Knowing, for Greek philosophy, was not *technē,* knowing how to do something; it was instead *wisdom,* knowledge of the self, of its structure or nature and its limits, and so knowledge of the eternal structures in which that nature of the self, in order to be fully itself, participates, becomes healed, and thus is enabled to become truly itself. It was, therefore, knowledge not merely of the objective interrelationships of things separated from the self, but precisely of the order inherent in the self itself; it thus quite reasonably led to wisdom or self-direction, and so to virtue. Modern knowing in science, on the other hand, is objective knowledge of external structures unrelated to the self, or to the mystery of its freedom. It thus totally overlooks the deeper problem of the self-control of the expert or the technologist even when he looks in himself and finds only benevolent ideals there—and so when it promises a modern version of Plato's ordered society, based on the wisdom of the intellectual elite, it appears almost ludicrously unconvincing.

If man's actions—even or perhaps especially when he has gained great power through his knowledge and is liberal and idealistic—remain ambiguous in basic motivation and often tragic in their unintended consequences, then such action must be undertaken and understood in terms of a deeper framework if it is to be creative. As we noted, a consciousness of this ambiguity, even of our own, is necessary if we are not to go blindly on doing the evil we never intended to do. Repentance in some sense is called for in every epoch—even in the bright new world the young scientists or the young radicals are bringing in for us. But then, when any generation, however secular, does finally see this fatal ambiguity, and the selfishness that was its cause, they are apt to find their moral nerve cut. An angry helplessness about any creative action anywhere appears—and men withdraw from social history in despair, disgust, and shame, as another wing of the younger generation now illustrates.

In every epoch of our history, then, we need to discover not only moral standards by which we may judge ourselves and the social world we live in, but also forgiveness somewhere for what we and our world are, and assurance of our ability to accept ourselves and our world, even in the ambiguity that we know to characterize them when we know the truth. Only thus are we enabled to go on with our worldly work for a better and juster world than we now have. And in order to do that, we need to have the faith that something works for good, even beyond and within the mess that we men have made and will continue to make. We need an intelligible ground for hope, a credible myth that does not lie to us about ourselves and our future. Finally, if life is in this way made up of ambiguity and frequent conflict, we need to have the urge for reconciliation with the others whom we have injured and with ourselves too.

All of this points beyond the scope and the capacities of our own knowledge and of our own moral powers to the deeper sources of both, the God who is creative of our astounding capacities, who judges our waywardness, and accepts our repentance; who works in the midst of our evil as well as of our good to further his purposes and fulfill his promises; and who calls us to reconciliation so that we may start again on his and our work for a better and more humane future. The vast new powers of science do not, in the end, make religious faith and commitment irrelevant; they make them more necessary than ever. And they make of the utmost importance the understanding and the use of the deeper symbols expressive of the real issues and so the real promises of man's destiny—the symbols of man's potentialities and nature as the image of God; of his waywardness as fallen from grace; of the judgment, the mercy, and the promise of God. Only on these terms can the mystery, the risk, and the promise of the destiny of a scientific culture be comprehended and borne.

Our argument has been that modern man has generated symbolic interpretations of his limits and his powers by which he understands himself and his hopes, but that these myths are contradictory and even dangerous, and above all quite unrelated to the facts of the case and therefore radically unempirical—ironical in an empirical culture such as ours. And we recommended in each case the Biblical symbolism about man, as first of all a creature amidst creatures, and so partially determined in his life, and yet secondly, as made in the image of God, and so free, creative, and rational, of intrinsic and ineradicable value, even when he is the patient in the backless hospital shift as well as the mighty doctor in the white coat! Further, that while he experiences within himself not only good intentions but also the freedom to enact them, nevertheless the strange fact is that these intentions get corrupted and warped—and thus his actual role in history is far more ambiguous than any modern myth contemplates. In this case the Biblical symbolism of sin and grace is again closer to the actual facts of the situation, and also expresses authentic rather than inauthentic grounds for confidence in the future.

The Grace and Hell of Technological Fate

Modern man, however, does not live on self-images alone. Although the cosmos is for him purposeless and therefore blind, nevertheless it is plain that he does count on aspects of objective process which help to guarantee to him a meaningful destiny or future. The first of these is the cumulative development of technology, of applied knowledge objectified, so to speak, in techniques, in instruments, tools, processes, and products. This represents an objective historical consequent of his own inner wisdom and virtue, the *way* in which evolution as a cumulative process "works" in culture and so in history—or so the myth tells us. Perhaps the central dream of modern scientific man has been that through this cumulative technology inclusive of techniques, attitudes, and products, he could save himself and his world: for technology is seen to represent the purest case of the victory of man's purposes over blind nature, of the supremacy of intentionality over chance. Where purposeless force once reigned, here now, in that bridge, that medical practice, this architectural wonder, those flying vehicles or industrial products, stand human uses of natural forces and materials for human purposes. Technology is thus the paradigm for the myth we are discussing, and it has transformed all of our lives in more helpful ways than we know—none of us would relinquish many of its benefits, especially the dishwasher!

And let us look more closely at technology. Ironically, it illustrates the deep ambiguity of all of man's powers and so of his history, combining possibilities for evil as well as for good, and even overlaying its own sources in our essential freedom with the necessitating cover of implacable fate. For technology itself has become one of the fates that haunt modern man, mocking his sense of control over himself and even over nature. In fact, it has almost replaced blind nature as the fate that threatens our contemporary existence—it is worse, more hazardous to health and safety, to live in cities than in nature; and the rapid uncontrolled development of technology frightens many thoughtful technologists to death.

Technology is a powerful modern symbol of the ambiguity of our destiny, if not of fate, for three reasons. Each of these reasons represents the loss of the control by man's rational and purposive intentionality over the technology that man has himself created. Thus has human freedom, in creating technology, warped itself into a fate that has become a threat precisely to that freedom. First, technology has the character of fate because the *fact* of the development or further expansion of technology cannot be stopped and is thus quite beyond human control. No political or moral force conceivable can prevent what is possible to be discovered and developed from being so; the further development of technology, whether we are pleased with its prospects or not, is as inevitable as any decree of the Greek Moira. New inventions, new developments in armaments, new improvements in industry, communications, and transport, are appearing at an accelerated pace from a thousand laboratories and for a thousand reasons, economic and political. Thus *as a whole* their appearance on the scene of history is in fact unintended and unplanned; ironically, it is more an example of the irrationality of past history than of the "planning" that was supposed to be characteristic of the technological future. As a consequence, when one looks at the rise and progress of technology itself, it is very hard to see how the word "decision," so often used by writers on the subject of the uses of science, applies even remotely here. Appearing thus quite without central or intentional control, the steady progress of technology obviously cannot be intentionally stopped; it is a fate about which man can do very little indeed.

Secondly, technology represents a modern form of fate because the shape or direction of this unstoppable expansion is also not under any measure of rational determination or control. The expansion of technology is literally a "frolic" of unplanned, arbitrary, and often trivial expansion. New products, processes, and instruments are hourly developed which may at best waste our resources and labor, at worst work untold harm on the environment, on the economy, or on man. And yet no rational planning or moral calculation of the direction of this expansion is even contemplated. The myth that technology can solve every problem technology creates is invoked to calm our questions about new products and processes—and so we go on heedlessly. The course of technology represents, therefore, the height of contemporary unfreedom, the point in our social existence where man, and so *we,* probably have *least* intentional control over the shape of our own destiny—for that destiny will be in large part determined by precisely this frolic of expansion. In political and economic life, not to mention the family future, ways have been worked out to reduce the utterly arbitrary character of our common march into tomorrow. Technology seems the least subject to such intentional control, and thus what it brings to us in the days to come seems more of a fate than is almost anything else in modern experience.

Finally, technology is a radical symbol for fate because the development and use of technology reveals itself to be the servant, not at all of our rational and moral wisdom, but rather of our bondage, that is, of our more sinful and greedy impulses—of the profit motive, of national pride, and of national and class paranoia. In history the image of man as creative manipulator of his destiny gets sadly muddied—as the stinging eyes and shortened breath of each modern technologist, coughing and gasping as he drives home from work through the smog, sadly illustrate.

Recently a second "objective" element has appeared in the modern understanding of destiny, one even stranger than the faith in the cumulative benefits of technology. Possibly because of our sense of the rapidity of technological change and even of the ambiguity of what it has produced, we have begun to wonder about the future: What will our destiny be like? Will it reveal the continuity of our values or their destruction? Is what we are building now really relative (as science seems to say) or is it a part of the permanent grain of things? And so we have begun to predict, not (like Nostradamus) as an errant, bizarre element of our culture but as a serious activity of the Establishment itself, represented by scientific publications and societies, a foundation for the future in Washington, and an official volume of *Daedalus* in the summer of 1967. Kooks like Ezekiel used to do this and salve our fevered nerves about the future; but now prediction has also become scientific, and so we can scientifically discern the shape of things to come. Thus, led by Herman Kahn and Albert Wiener, does a scientific society replace another traditional function of the religious seer and in scientific terms answer our anxious questions about destiny.

Here, let me suggest, the second mythical base for our confidence appears. Every prediction, at least in the issue of *Daedalus* devoted to the year 2000,[8] assumed two invariables without which scientific prediction would have been impossible. First, each began with a telltale phrase "assuming that long-term trends continue," a reasonable enough assumption in a scientific culture oriented in nature (does not the sun rise each day?) but utterly question-begging about history. What would a survey of southern prospects have been had it been conducted in 1856 in Richmond—assuming that the long-term trends in the life of Virginia would continue? or prospects in the Berlin or Vienna of 1912? The trends represented by the Hapsburg empire and the Prussian monarchy were indeed "long-term"—but they were about to evaporate in the mysterious twists of history. So also, shudderingly enough, may it be with our culture's long-term trends! To assume that our favorite trends, which have brought us into being and preserve us there, will continue is *already* to answer the basic question of historical prediction. It makes us feel good, to be sure—but is it scientific or even rational? No, it is sheer myth, and bad myth at that, for it has neither empirical nor rational bases in an understanding of the character of historical process.

Second, each prediction assumed as the other variable the existence in the year 2000 of what was called "a free society"—and what a relief that was to one worried by Orwell and Huxley! What each man did, therefore, was apparently to ask himself (*a*) what would a free society look like if (*b*) present long-term trends continue and are extrapolated another thirty years hence? Clearly, without these two invariables no prediction is possible—unless Hosea or Ezekiel were called in! But with these two assumptions, all our outstanding questions have in fact already been answered. In fact, instead of penetrating by scientific wisdom and mathematical prediction the mystery of the future, what we have done is precisely to assume that mystery away—and then, having assumed it away, of course to predict along the straight sure track of the continuance of our present cultural life! If only destiny were that secure.

As is quite apparent here, modern scientific culture stares into the same opaque future as has any culture, and it is just as fearful and unsure of the destiny that awaits it. The only difference is that we fully believe we can resolve this mystery of our destiny—as we had the mystery of our freedom—through our scientific know-how. In both cases we show ourselves to be superficial and even silly, less empirically related to the reality of facts than most previous cultures. Clearly, on the deeper levels of our life our culture is more naïve than many another that preceded it, our symbols are self-contradictory and unrelated to reality, vulnerable to the least rational or skeptical questioning. Compared with these brittle symbolic interpretations of man's freedom and his destiny, our traditional Biblical symbols of God's Providence, his faithfulness, and his promises of a creative new age to come make much more sense. Ezekiel had more rational bases for his predictions about the mystery of the future than does Herman Kahn!

In What Can Man Hope?

Man cannot become the arbiter of his own destiny without intellectual contradiction and historical self-destruction. If he is to have confidence in his destiny, therefore, he must recapture that sense of the creativity, wonder, and sacrality of the given, as the source and ground of his own powers, of his potentialities, and so of his hopes. He must understand the present and the future course of his history as not just the *servant* of his autonomy and creativity, but also that in a mysterious way his history mediates to him his rightful *Lord*. Judgment on his own misuse of his powers and grace to re-create them must be mediated to him through his destiny if he is to have any confidence at all. The more he understands empirically the mystery of his own freedom, the more ambiguous and fearful to him will the destiny that science presents to him become. All that more knowledge can do is to increase our freedom and thus to increase the ambiguity that opens out in the future use of our powers. Science does not answer the ultimate question of human hope. It raises that question more poignantly than ever. An examination, therefore, of the uses of science reveals that inescapably, if we are to understand our future in the light of scientific knowledge, we must move our reflection, and so our language, to the relations of human freedom—however increased—to sin, to judgment, and to renewal. And so finally we must begin to think of the entire eschatological scope of the work of Divine Grace in history. The dilemmas of even the most secular of cultures are intelligible only in the light of faith; the destiny of even a scientific world can be thematized only in terms of religious symbols; and the confidence for the future even of technological man can only be grounded if the coming work of the Lord in the affairs of men is known and affirmed.

To sum up our theme, every image of man points beyond itself to an ultimate horizon of being within which that image takes its place—it is theological as well as anthropological—it entails a cosmic and historical myth as well as a view of man. If nature, as secular culture sees it, is truly blind and pointless, then man himself takes on this sacral ultimacy and absoluteness, and sees himself as free and wise, as the Promethean godlet who can control history for his own ends and thus creates meaning and value *ex nihilo* out of the blindness of process. Such a pessimistic view of being and optimistic view of man is, we have argued, self-contradictory and unempirical, and thus doomed to collapse at the slightest breath of reality.

If, therefore, we take a more realistic view of man as both free and determined, as both virtuous and ambiguous, good and sinful —as he is—then inevitably the grounds for historical hope, on which we all depend, must shift their balance, and, as in most human schemes of meaning, a cosmic, ontological ground of hope is discerned to balance the more realistic view of man. This by no means proves that there is a God, or an ultimate order or scheme to history and social process. These cannot be proved. They can only be discerned by deep, involved intuition, by an apprehension of the wonder and meaning of the given structure of things in which our own reality and our own waywardness fit and find their place. But that discernment or faith can arise, I believe, when we begin where we have begun: with a critical look at our images of man. And in that discernment of a wider sacral context of our human story, we can find grounds beyond our own intelligence and virtue for a hopeful answer to the question of our destiny. The immediate foreground of our destiny is, to be sure, dominated by our waxing powers of knowledge and control. Nevertheless, the horizon of our future is as shrouded in mystery as in any other age, for the ambiguity of our freedom and our fate, and the strange way they can interact in history, remain as impenetrable as ever, giving to our feelings for the future the deep tone of anxiety. In our age, as in any other, therefore, confidence and hope depend upon a sense of the transcendent Lord of all things—for unless the Lord builds the house, the builders do labor in vain.

NOTES

1. Cf. the remarkable discussion of modern "scientific myths," i.e., myths whose origins lay in scientific inquiry but whose latter-day meanings have become that of religious myth, by Stephen Toulmin, "Contemporary Scientific Mythology," in A. McIntyre (ed.), *Metaphysical Beliefs* (London: SCM Press Ltd., 1957), pp. 13–61.

2. Cf. Peter Gay, *The Enlightenment: An Interpretation* (Alfred A. Knopf, Inc., 1967), pp. 148–150 and 419.

3. George Gaylord Simpson, *The Meaning of Evolution* (Mentor Book, The New American Library, Inc., 1957), pp. 155–156.

4. Theodosius Dobzhansky, *Mankind Evolving* (Yale University Press, 1962), pp. 346–347.

5. Victor C. Ferkiss, *Technological Man* (George Braziller, Inc., 1969), p. 111.

6. Quoted in *ibid.*, pp. 20–21.

7. Julian H. Steward, "Cultural Evolution Today," in K. Haselden and P. J. Hefner (eds.), *Changing Man: The Threat and the Promise* (Doubleday & Company, Inc., 1967), pp. 50–51.

8. *Daedalus,* "Toward the Year 2000: Work in Progress," Vol. 96, No. 3 (Summer, 1967).

CHAPTER V

A Psychologist's View
of Good and Evil
and the Church of the Future

O. H. Mowrer

Is man inherently good? Is he inherently evil? Or is he neither—an amoral, ethically neutral creature? Despite many recent attempts to show that morality cannot be defined precisely or investigated scientifically and is therefore a meaningless problem, we go right ahead talking about virtue and evil, and judging conduct, both our own and that of others, as good or bad. So it would seem that, at the outset, we can eliminate the supposition that man is morally indifferent, ethically insensitive, amoral. Instead, we must apparently posit that for him morality is a vital, relevant, and enduring concern. This, then, reduces the issue, as originally formulated, to a dichotomy: Is man inherently good or inherently evil?

A lively debate usually ensues whenever one assumes and defends one of these alternatives as against the other. But we will, it seems, be on sounder ground if we take the position that there are inherent tendencies in human beings which dispose us all toward *both* good and evil. These tendencies, as I shall try to show, are deeply rooted in human nature, and there are strong forces propelling man toward virtue but also pulling him toward evil. Although we may not believe in the formal doctrines of original sin and the substitutionary atonement, the inescapable fact seems to be that man is an original and recurrent sinner and always will be; but he is also capable of creativity and originality in finding ways of extricating himself from sin and working out his own salvation. Thus, we may say man is perennially disposed toward goodness, wisdom, and virtue, as well as toward evil, stupidity, and folly.

If these reflections are valid, it follows that life must always be lived in the context of a certain amount of tension and strain; and although there are personal strategies and life-styles which will lessen or increase this tension, it can never be altogether eliminated. So we may say that all men have the *capacity* for both good and evil; and, to paraphrase a common proverb, we may add that there is some good in the worst of us and some evil in the best of us. The problem, then, practically speaking, is how to capitalize on our propensities for goodness and self-control and minimize our susceptibility to temptation and evil.

The "Fall of Man" and the Problems of Evil

That man's struggle with good and evil has been perennial and ancient is indicated by the fact that early in the first book of the Old Testament, known as Genesis, there is a great allegory revolving around the tree of life and the tree of the knowledge of good and evil. This allegory is sometimes referred to simply as the "story of the fall of man." According to this story, Adam, the first man, could eat freely all the fruits that abounded in the Garden of Eden, except one: "Of the tree of the knowledge of good and evil," said the Lord of Creation, "you shall not eat, for in the day that you eat of it you shall die."

We are, of course, familiar with how the Lord then decided that Adam should have a companion and created a woman for him, known as Eve. Then, as the story goes on to tell us, a serpent appeared and persuaded the woman to eat of the forbidden fruit, with the promise: "When you eat of it your eyes will be opened, and you will be like God, knowing good and evil." The woman ate of the fruit of the tree of the knowledge of good and evil and persuaded her husband to do so; and although both then knew the difference between good and evil, they were rendered not serene and godlike but guilty, ashamed, and miserable. Thus they lost their original ethical ignorance and innocence; and, lest Adam and Eve should now also eat of the tree of life and become immortal, they were cast out of the Garden of Eden into the world as we know it today—and as ordinary human beings have always known it: with a longing for goodness and peace but also a susceptibility to sin and misery.

This was the superb, figurative way in which the ancient Hebrews conceptualized the problem of good and evil. But because many of us no longer take this story literally but dismiss it as "mythical," does this mean that the problem of good and evil is no longer with us, that we can renounce all issues of morality and thus escape the experience of evil and guilt? By no means! So it will perhaps be useful if we can recast the problem in more contemporary, albeit less dramatic, terms.

A Simple Geometrical Model

Perhaps we can usefully reformulate the problem of good and evil by posing the following question: If goodness is really good—and good *for* us, why do we sometimes act badly, with undesirable, indeed often disastrous, consequences? In short, why should the problem of evil, that is, of bad, self-defeating behavior, exist?

There is a diagram that I find illuminating in this connection, which consists of a simple right triangle. Imagine the right angle of the triangle composed of a horizontal line running from right to left and there joining with a perpendicular vertical line of the same length extending downward. Let us call the vertical line AB and the horizontal line BC. The hypotenuse of the triangle will thus be AC.

Let us now suppose that we are at A and our objective is to get from A to C. Obviously, the shortest path from A to C is the hypotenuse of the triangle. But often "morality" says that we shall not go from A to C by this route but that we shall take the longer route ABC. Immediately a conflict arises. We can readily see that the shortest, quickest route from A to C is along the hypotenuse of the triangle, but the "rules," the principles of right and wrong, say that we must make this journey by the longer route ABC.

So our dilemma is: Shall we be good and take the longer path or shall we disobey the rules and "do what comes naturally," namely, take the quick and easy route?

Before we proceed further with our analysis of this type of situation, let me concretize it in two ways. The situation may be simply that of a lawn, where the perpendicular sides of the triangle represent a sidewalk and where there is beautiful grass which the hypotenuse or path AC would cross. There may be a sign in this situation which says: "Please do not walk on the grass." In other words, the bad consequences, or evil, that would result if we went from A to C along the hypotenuse of the triangle would be that we would soon destroy some of the grass by walking on it and would disfigure the lawn. And if we disregarded the sign and walked on the grass, we might be shouted at by the proprietor of the lawn or we might even be arrested, whereas if we remained on the sidewalk, we could "go in peace."

Another simple illustration of this way of distinguishing between right and wrong would be the following: Let us suppose that C represents not a point in space but a goal of another kind, for example, that of money. Now, the "rules" say that the proper way to get money is to *work* for it, and that involves, figuratively, taking the longer, harder route represented by the perpendicular lines AB, BC in the triangle. What would the alternative route AC involve in this case? It might involve burglary, forgery, swindling, or some more violent activity, such as armed robbery or perhaps even murder. This, we would say, was a bad, immoral, evil, or criminal solution to the problem; yet some people at least periodically or perhaps habitually take route AC when they want money, instead of getting it in the good, approved way, by taking route ABC, which involves *working* for it.

From these and innumerable other examples which could be given, it is clear that some human beings are good, or at least predominantly so, whereas other human beings are bad, at least a part—perhaps a very large part—of the time. So the *fact* of good and bad conduct is obvious and ubiquitous and needs no elaborate documentation or argument. This conclusion does not, however, answer our question: Is man *inherently* good or evil? It merely indicates that human beings sometimes act virtuously and sometimes otherwise, and that both good and bad behavior are human realities; and the geometrical illustration helps us specify and clarify what we mean, in principle, when we refer to conduct that is good and conduct that is evil.

Intelligence and the Problem of Good and Evil

At first blush it might appear that the problem of good and evil could easily be resolved in terms of intelligence and stupidity. Good behavior, as we have thus far analyzed it, seems eminently rational, intelligent; and bad behavior seems grossly stupid and self-defeating. A popular—or perhaps I should say, a *once* popular slogan—says: "Crime doesn't pay," with the implicit injunction, "so don't be a chump and engage in it." But crime and evil persist, so the rationality argument is by no means axiomatic to everyone and apparently to some persons is itself stupid and "irrational."

The difficulty with the rationality approach to good and evil solutions to problems is that each, in its own way, is both intelligent *and* stupid. A good person is intelligent in that he characteristically reaches his goals in such a way that other persons do not object to or interfere with his behavior and he is not criticized or punished; but he is "stupid" if I may use that term, in a rather special sense, in that he chooses an arduous and slow way of gratifying his needs and wishes in preference to quick and easy ones. The evil person, on the other hand, chooses exactly the opposite strategy, which, again, involves both an intelligent and a stupid aspect. His behavior is intelligent in that he typically goes to his goals by the quickest and easiest methods; that is, he takes what we call shortcuts (which, in many situations are regarded as insights, creative innovations, inventions, etc.). But the shortcuts which the man of evil takes are of such a nature that, if known to others, they are likely to precipitate rebuke or, in more serious cases, personal retaliation or perhaps legal action; and if these shortcut solutions are carried out by stealth, their perpetrator is always in danger of being found out and is thus rendered more or less chronically insecure, furtive, apprehensive.

On the other hand, there *are* situations where taking a shortcut may involve insight, creativity, or adaptive "reality testing." Imagine that for a prehistoric tribe the route from *A* to *C* was taboo because a saber-toothed tiger lived in a cave along the way. But then further suppose that someday one or more persons were so rash (*or* "courageous") as nevertheless to take path *AC* and they found that the tiger was dead and that the formerly dangerous path was now safe. This illustrates the adage that "circumstances alter cases" and shows that what may once have been bad, evil, stupid, is now safe and desirable. This thought is capsulated in one line of a poem by James Russell Lowell (often sung as a hymn) which, if I recall correctly, reads: "Time makes ancient good uncouth." But the dependence of a moral truth upon circumstances does not lessen its relevance and urgency if the circumstances are of one sort rather than another.

This, I suppose, might be interpreted as a form of "situation ethics," as indeed it is. But I feel that Joseph Fletcher[1] has carried his argument to an absurdity—and interest in it seems, appropriately, to be gradually declining. In his book he seems to be saying that there should be no rules whatever, and that every situation should be treated, so to say, on its own merits—"decided in love," to use one of his favorite expressions. Suppose, to take a simple but highly pertinent example, that there were no "rules of the road" and that each time two cars approached from opposite directions, the drivers had to take time out to decide whether to pass one another on the right or on the left. The result would not be freedom but confusion and chaos of the worst sort. Rules are not made to "hold us down" but to help us get to our "destinations" in the quickest and easiest way that is compatible with the common good. Rules may indeed become outmoded (as seems to be happening today with regard to certain traditional sexual mores), but this does not mean that rules are *never* desirable, useful, and worthy of our fullest observance and loyalty. A society without rules, general agreements, "contracts," would be a shambles, a nonsociety.[2]

The Role of Time and the Concept of Net Gain

It thus becomes evident that we cannot resolve the problem of good and evil, in any very simple or obvious way, by saying that one is intelligent, smart, and the other unintelligent, stupid. Both approaches to the solution of life's moral problems involve intelligent *and* stupid aspects—or, said a little differently, both involve advantages and disadvantages. How is this dilemma to be resolved? I am sure that, at this juncture, many of you will have already found yourselves introducing, in your own minds, the *time* dimension, and this enables us to take a substantial step toward the resolution of the dilemma. Already we have established that evil and virtue involve both advantages and disadvantages, but we must now notice also that there is a difference in the *ordering* or *timing* of the consequences thereof. By and large, we can say that in the case of evil solutions to problems, the advantages come quickly and the disadvantages tend to be delayed (or sometimes, in the overt sense of the wrongdoer's being caught and punished, averted altogether), whereas, in the case of good solutions to moral problems, the disadvantages come first and the advantages or "payoff" tends to be delayed (or, again, in an unstable or unjust situation, it may not materialize at all). In other words, virtue, like evil, always involves a risk or gamble, but a gamble of a different sort: the evil person, by his impulsive action, insures impulse gratification, but at the risk of being, sooner or later, punished, whereas the good person "controls himself" and works and waits, but may or may not receive his just rewards.

If time were the only factor involved here, we would all surely be perpetual sinners, sociopaths, criminals—that is, persons habitually given to resorting to so-called bad rather than good solutions to moral problems. For who wants a delayed satisfaction of a need if an equally good one is available immediately? We have already said that good solutions take more time and effort than do evil ones, so the balance would be heavily in favor of bad rather than good solutions. That is to say, "good" solutions to problems would be *bad* and "bad" solutions to problems would be *good*. But manifestly, things do not work this way; and in order to explain why they do not, we have to take not only time and effort into account but also a factor which can perhaps be best termed "net gain." In a bad solution to a problem, although the goal is typically reached quickly and easily, there are likely to be delayed negative consequences which are *more punishing* than the quick-and-easy goal attainment was rewarding or satisfying. On the other hand, in a *good* instance of goal attainment, although more time and effort are involved in "getting there" than in the case of a bad problem-solving strategy, there are not likely to be any delayed negative consequences, and the satisfaction ultimately achieved is more than worth what it has cost in terms of the sacrifices required to achieve it.[3]

Thus we arrive at a rather interesting conclusion: namely, that good behavior is good because the *total satisfaction* experienced over time tends to outweigh the requisite energy expenditure and gratification postponement, and bad behavior is bad because the *total experienced satisfaction* tends to be *less* than what it ultimately costs. Thus good behavior turns out to be intelligent and in one's long-term self-interest, and bad behavior turns out to be stupid and self-defeating, in the slightly complicated way which has been explained. Was it not Socrates who long ago argued that in the final analysis virtue and wisdom are the same? And there are contemporary empirical studies which show that the results of intelligence tests and objective measures of morality are positively correlated.[4]

The Role of "Authority," Temporal and Supernatural, in the Control of Behavior

Although good behavior is, by definition and in reality, in the long run preferable to bad behavior from a purely hedonistic, self-fulfilling standpoint, the fact is that human beings, when very young, are typically impulsive rather than controlled and prudent in their pursuit of pleasure and only gradually learn to be "good," and that no one is ever wholly immune to the lure of temptation, that is, the tendency, on occasion, to revert from virtuous and wise action to evil and foolish action.[5] And it has long been recognized that human beings *need help* in their pursuit of goodness. In the case of infants and children this help comes from the concern, discipline, and "authority" which their parents (or parental surrogates) in all societies exercise over them; and when human beings become adult, if they are to live together in any sort of harmony and productiveness, they must be subject to some sort of external force or power, the exercise of which is the prerogative of the chief in tribal situations, of kings in autocratic societies, and of duly constituted "public officials" in democratic societies. In all of these instances, it is the *duty* of persons "in authority" to keep the peace by seeing to it that individuals, when they lack the inner capacity to behave themselves, do so out of fear of external coercion, loss of privileges, or punishment.

But, being human themselves, such authorities cannot, or do not, always execute their duties perfectly in this connection; and mankind has a long history of resorting to supernatural powers in its struggle toward virtue and against evil. In Sumner and Keller's now somewhat dated but nevertheless still monumental work entitled *The Science of Society,* the problem is set forth, graphically and colorfully, in the following words:

Not without justice has it been written that fear is the beginning of knowledge. It is certainly the beginning of that discipline through which alone wisdom arrives. Discipline was precisely what men needed in the childhood of the race and have continued to require ever since. Men must learn to control themselves. Though the regulative organization exercised considerable discipline, its agents were merely human; the chief had to sleep occasionally, could not be everywhere at once, and might be deceived and evaded. Not so the ghosts and spirits. The all-seeing daimonic eye was sleepless; no time or place was immune from its surveillance. Detection was sure. Further, the penalty inflicted was awesome. Granted that the chief might beat or maim or fine or kill, there were yet limits to what he could do. The spirits, on the other hand, could inflict strange agonies and frightful malformations and transformations. Their powers extended even beyond the grave and their resources for harm outran the liveliest imaginings. In short, they inspired, not a daylight-fear but a grisly, gruesome terror—ghost-fear. Consider the threat of the taboo, and its effectiveness. It is beneath this unearthly whip of scorpions that humanity has cringed for long ages and there is no doubt that its disciplinary value has superseded all other compulsions to which mankind has ever been subject.[6]

Today I can recall, clearly and with some discernment, the span of more than half a century of life in our society; and I remember that when I was eleven or twelve years old, there was a book in our family library (housed in the small, glass-enclosed "bookcase" in our "parlor") which fascinated me far more than any of the other rarely consulted volumes there. As I remember it, this book had very little text and was made up largely of pictures (actually engravings) of the devil carrying out his varied and far-reaching responsibilities on earth and in hell. Although he was a terrible-looking fellow, he did not seem, to my youthful eyes at least, altogether unlikable or unhappy. And this much was certain: he took his work very seriously and gave every indication of enjoying it. Stated most generally, the devil's primary duty on earth was to *tempt* living mortals and to superintend the punishment in hell of those who yielded to his blandishments and failed to repent soon enough. On Sundays, the ministers of the Protestant church which my family and I regularly attended pictured hell to us even more vividly than did the book (in color and with sound effects) and assured us that the fires burned brightly and that the place was doing a thriving business. But our ministers, for some reason, did not seem to want to appear to know too much about the general overseer of this institution—perhaps this is why I found our old book, appropriately bound in red, so uniquely instructive and interesting. Our ministers also, of course, discoursed on heaven—and were much freer to talk about God, whose supreme objective was to help human beings *be good* in this life so they could share eternity with him.

It now appears, in retrospect, that by roughly 1920, the devil was failing to command full credence, rather generally—which was, from one point of view, a grave misfortune; for if he was allowed to disappear from the minds of men, it was predictable that the fires of hell would cool and the place itself would eventually disappear. I have, of course, no way of knowing just how rapidly this indeed happened—I have often thought how instructive it would be if we had available today the results of a Gallop poll taken, let us say, at five-year intervals, during the half century between 1920 and 1970, on the decline of "belief" in this general area. But it seems fairly certain that the devil went first, and then hell likewise gradually faded into oblivion.

Hell's obsolescence was officially recognized in theological circles when E. Stanley Jones announced that "hell is portable," that is, that it is a human condition and not a place. And if our assumption is correct that man himself is *both* good and evil, we could have predicted that if this personal and spatial way of representing evil and its fruits disappeared, heaven and God would also be endangered. Sometime in the 1950's, I recall hearing a sermon entitled "What's Happened to Heaven?" Suddenly I said to myself: "As a matter of fact, you don't hear much about heaven anymore, do you?" The dissolution of hell had, it seems, created an unnatural imbalance. With this "institution" gone, everyone now presumably went to heaven; and if this were the case, the whole "other world" arrangement seemed rather pointless. Furthermore, about the same time, the existentialists descended upon us with the revelation that, as a matter of fact, no one was "going" anywhere! Tillich's terms "human finitude" and "our creatureliness" became household expressions, all of which left God without a permanent address and, as someone observed, "largely unemployed." Small wonder that it was only a few years until the "rumor" that God was dead had developed into a vigorous, if somewhat paradoxical, "theological movement," which was launched by Vahanian's book[7] and has been "reviewed" by Adolfs.[8] Today it is generally conceded that our society is basically secular[9] and that the "three-storied universe" of traditional Christianity is "mythical."[10]

The sequential process whereby this scheme of supernatural entities and sanctions disappeared from the modern scene thus seems to have been: first to go was the devil, then hell, then heaven, and finally—at least in any naïvely anthropomorphic sense—God. Many of us recall that if, as children, we asked *why* this or that act was bad, we were likely to be told either that God did not *want* us to perform it or that the devil would *get* us if we did. It is, therefore, perhaps not surprising that the disappearance of the "all-seeing, sleepless daimonic eye" and its accouterments has also badly shaken our faith in and respect for many human institutions which have claimed support and authentication from divine sources. For more than a decade now, we have been in an acute moral crisis, uncertain and confused as to where we can look for moral clarity and reliable guidance to the good life. In the earlier sections of this chapter, some suggestions have been put forward as to how we can reapproach the problem of good and evil, in an entirely objective, naturalistic, humanistic frame of reference. In the next and concluding section we shall take a look at certain enterprises which are specifically interested in putting such a conceptual approach into practice.

The Probable Shape of Things to Come in Character Development and Nurture

It is not without significance, surely, that the institution or movement which is today most effective in producing personal *change* in adult human beings is one which (*a*) has no truck with any form of supernaturalism and (*b*) does not even use the traditional terminology of secular ethical theory. I refer to Synanon Foundation, whose "houses" are located mainly in major cities on the West Coast and whose specialty is the rehabilitation of hardcore drug addicts. Here there is, officially, no prayer or worship in the conventional sense, and even the terms "good" and "bad" are generally eschewed. Instead, behavior is likely to be characterized as *smart* or *stupid,* in the self-actualizing, self-defeating, selfishly hedonic sense previously discussed. That the power and effectiveness of this approach lie not in the personal charisma of Synanon's founder, Charles Dederich, but in clearly articulated principles and processes[11] is indicated by the fact that a very similar organization, known as Daytop Village, Inc., has come into existence in New York City and is now spreading up and down the Atlantic seaboard.[12] Both organizations owe much of their inspiration and know-how to Alcoholics Anonymous, which specializes in another admittedly "impossible" task, namely, the rehabilitation of alcoholics.

Being neither an addict nor an alcoholic, I have had only tangential (but very cordial) contact with Synanon, Daytop, and AA; but I have been persuaded for a full quarter of a century now that functional personality disorders or so-called neuroses are intrinsically associated with basically moral problems and their persistent mismanagement. This conviction eventuated first in what was called "integrity therapy"[13]; but the name, and the process for which it stood, was attractive only to persons who were actively "hurting," and when they became reasonably comfortable, they, sensibly enough, disappeared. Who needs "therapy" if he is no longer "sick"? But we are now seeing the problem increasingly in educational rather than medical terms and have therefore dropped the term "therapy" and speak only of *"integrity groups."* As a result of this and related changes, people are now coming into our groups and *staying,* not because they are "still hurting," but because their pain has turned to a form of joy, which they feel they can continue to experience in no other way. In our groups, *personal change* and a form of *special training* go hand in hand. As a person becomes increasingly comfortable as a result of such change, he also begins to take deep satisfaction in new competences and skills which can then be exercised *in behalf of others.*

This is not the place to speak at length about integrity groups.[14] But this much is pertinent: we believe that these groups, as a facet of what is coming to be known, generally, as the small-groups movement, represent the emergence of a new *primary social institution.* In an era when the traditional primary social groups—home, church, school, and community—are badly shaken and confused, it is increasingly difficult for many persons to find identity, intimacy, emotional support, and cosmic meaning. It seems that the small-groups movement, of which integrity groups are one facet, represents an increasingly successful effort, on the part of more and more people, to avoid anonymity, alienation, and despair. The part of this movement with which I am most closely associated has frankly moral or ethical objectives: to help oneself and others to become more *honest, responsible,* and *emotionally involved.* And *help* in the attainment or at least approximation of these objectives is found in the hope of heaven and the fear of hell, not as places but as human conditions in this life.

Recently there has been an unprecedented upsurge of interest in small groups, which has been reflected, among other ways, by the fact that several large-circulation magazines have run very thoughtful and competently written articles on this phenomenon. A long list of such articles could be cited, but one will suffice: namely, a piece by Sam Blum entitled, "Group Therapy: A Special Report."[15] Personally, I think there is a good possibility that these groups represent the emerging form of the church of the twenty-first century. They will very likely differ from conventional Catholic and Protestant churches in that they will not be specifically Christocentric, nor will they be explicitly theistic (compare Confucianism and Buddhism). But they will, I think, be *profoundly religious.* This may seem like a contradiction in terms to some, who will ask: "But how can anyone be religious without also believing in God?" The answer is very simple. The term "religion," in its literal derivation, has no necessary relation to "theology." The former term comes from the Latin root *ligare,* which means "connection"; and *re-ligare,* from which our term "religion" comes, means "reconnection." And this, more than perhaps anything else, is what the small-groups movement is concerned with: the reconnection, reintegration, reconciliation of lost, lonely, isolated, alienated, estranged persons back into a loving, concerned, and orderly fellowship or group of some sort.

Dietrich Bonhoeffer was apparently envisioning something of this kind when toward the end of his life,[16] he spoke about "man coming of age" and of a "religionless Christianity." But his choice of terms was, I think, unfortunate. We would prefer to speak of a "nontheistic religion," of the sort which one already sees explicitly embodied in many forms of contemporary small groups. Yet in one sense there is a striking continuity and kinship here between the contemporary small-groups movement and Christianity. The early or apostolic church was basically a small-groups movement and was based, not in churches as we know them today, but typically in individual homes, where a "congregation" would consist of perhaps only ten or a dozen persons; and when the group got larger than this, it would divide and provide the nucleus of two new groups. Thus the early church was also known as a house church; and when, as in Rome, it was not safe to meet in private homes, these little bands found refuge and a degree of safety in the catacombs. Here honesty (confession, exomologesis), responsibility (restitution, penance), and involvement (loving-kindness) were all practiced, with the same salubrious effects we see them capable of producing today. But there is, of course, the very significant difference that the small groups ("congregations," "house churches") with which we are here particularly concerned are naturalistic and humanistic, rather than metaphysical and theistic, in their basic orientation.

And why do human beings continue to need "religious" groups, regardless of their cosmology or world view? Because, as previously noted in this chapter, we all need help in pursuing the good and avoiding evil. Socially isolated, estranged man is weak and highly prone to evil, self-defeating behavior. Bonhoeffer, in his book *Life Together,* puts it this way: "In confession the breakthrough to community takes place. Sin demands to have a man by himself. It withdraws him from the community. The more isolated a person is, the more destructive will be the power of sin over him, and the more deeply he becomes involved in it, the more disastrous is his isolation. Sin wants to remain unknown. It shuns the light. In the darkness of the unexpressed it poisons the whole being of a person."[17]

The most reliable means yet discovered for obtaining help in overcoming estrangement and building resistance to temptation ("ego strength") comes from commitment to and earnest participation in a properly conceived and contractually structured group of fellow human beings, that is, of one's *peers.* The best safeguard of legal rights and justice ever evolved is probably the principle, in English law, of the "right to trial before a jury of one's peers"; and it is no accident that the kinds of small groups discussed in this chapter are now being commonly referred to as "peer self-help groups."[18]

Today there is manifestly widespread uncertainty, conflict, and pain in the area of morality and "values." This is perhaps the price we have to pay as we move through a religious "reformation" which, in historical retrospect, may prove to be far more important, sounder, and unifying than that of the sixteenth century.

NOTES

1. Joseph Fletcher, *Situation Ethics: The New Morality* (The Westminster Press, 1966).

2. O. H. Mowrer, "Conflict, Contract, Conscience, and Confession," *Transactions* 1 (1969), pp. 17–19; see also Joseph Fletcher, *Moral Responsibility: Situation Ethics at Work* (The Westminster Press, 1967).

3. See O. H. Mowrer and A. D. Ullman, "Time as a Determinant in Integrative Learning," *Psychological Review* 52 (1945), pp. 61–90.

4. See, for example, Clara F. Chassell, *The Relation Between Morality and Intellect: A Compendium of Evidence Contributed by Psychology, Criminology, and Sociology* (Bureau of Publications, Teachers College, Columbia University, 1935).

5. See the distinction made by Freud, in 1911, between the Pleasure Principle and the Reality Principle, in "Formulations Regarding Two Principles of Mental Function," *Collected Papers* (London: Hogarth Press, 1934), Vol. 4, pp. 13–21.

6. W. B. Sumner and A. G. Keller, *Self-Maintenance Religion,* Vol. 2 of *The Science of Society* (Yale University Press, 1927), pp. 1478–1479.

7. Gabriel Vahanian, *The Death of God* (George Braziller, Inc., 1961).

8. Robert Adolfs, *The Grave of God: Has the Church a Future?* (Harper & Row, Publishers, Inc., 1967).

9. See Harvey Cox, *The Secular City* (The Macmillan Company, 1965).

10. See the writings of Rudolf Bultmann in Hans W. Bartsch (ed.), *Kerygma and Myth: A Theological Debate,* tr. R. H. Fuller (London: S.P.C.K., 1953), Vol. I, pp. 1–44; see also William Hordern,

Introduction, Vol. I of *New Directions in Theology Today* (The Westminster Press, 1966), Ch. 2.

11. See, for example, Lewis Yablonsky, *The Tunnel Back: Synanon* (The Macmillan Company, 1965).

12. See J. A. Shelly and A. Bassin, "Daytop Lodge: A New Treatment Approach for Drug Addicts," *Corrective Psychiatry* 11 (1965), pp. 186–195; see also A. Bassin, "Daytop Village," *Psychology Today,* December, 1968, pp. 48 ff.

13. See, for example, J. W. Drakeford, *Integrity Therapy: A Christian Evaluation to a New Approach to Mental Health* (Broadman Press, 1967).

14. See, for example, O. H. Mowrer, "Integrity Groups Today" (mimeographed, Department of Psychology, University of Illinois, 1969).

15. *Redbook,* March, 1970, p. 134.

16. Dietrich Bonhoeffer, *Prisoner for God: Letters and Papers from Prison,* ed. by Eberhard Bethage, tr. by Reginald H. Fuller (The Macmillan Company, 1953).

17. Dietrich Bonhoeffer, *Life Together,* tr. by J. W. Doberstein (Harper & Brothers, 1954), p. 112.

18. See N. Hurvitz, "The Characteristics of Peer Self-Help Psychotherapy Groups and Their Implications for the Theory and Practice of Psychotherapy," *Psychotherapy: Theory, Research, and Practice* 7 (1970), pp. 41–49.

CHAPTER VI

Science
and the Quest for Human Values

Robert L. Sinsheimer

In time it will probably be seen as inevitable that science, which set out simply to explore the universe objectively—without the constraints of, indeed orthogonal to, the concerns of value—should have come to test in the harshest way the fabric of our values. Today it takes little vision to see that science is ready to pose to man wholly unprecedented questions of the most fundamental character which will of necessity require a reformulation and a deeper understanding of our basic moral principles.

For us in science, it is frankly still surprising to have come from a new direction upon the oldest of questions. Perhaps, as we reflect, this consequence will tell us something about the geometry of fate and the matrix of the human mind.

We are already confronted with grave dilemmas arising from the only partial triumphs of science, which splinter our older values and often expose their expedience and inconsistency. The Malthusian tide of population mocks our belief in the value of individual man; the flood of factual knowledge overwhelms our faith in the immanent value of truth and thrusts us in the feckless role of the sorcerer's apprentice; the disintegration by death undermines our ancient views of the beneficent role of the healer and the worth of human life. Graver questions yet lie ahead as the biological sciences prepare to change the boundary conditions of man.

Herbert Simon has recently proposed what he calls the science of the artificial, as distinct from the science of the natural. The latter is concerned with the analysis, the reduction to comprehension, of things as they are. The former is concerned with the analysis of the means for the achievement of purpose, for the fulfillment of preset goals. In this context, we need also a third category of science—what we might call the science of the existential —which will have as its concern the choice of goals for human existence, the coherent illumination and the clear definition of purpose for the lives of this very special creature, man.

What could be the relation of natural science to such an existential science—can natural science inform the quest for human values? I believe it can in many ways and I will hope to illustrate a few of these. Conversely, the quest for values can inform science of the directions in which factual knowledge and unifying concepts are most urgently needed for the resolution of our mounting crises.

There is first a fundamental distinction to be made. The quest for value is ultimately an enterprise in synthesis. Almost all of our properly vaunted science is analysis—the dissociation and understanding of the world of nature, as it is given to us. The recent decipherment of the genetic code was a brilliant and an epochal achievement, but the code was there long before man and only in the most limited sense did we invent it.

But values are, for the larger part, man-made. They must derive from the remarkable circumstance that a new phenomenon has, in the long course of time, emerged upon this planet—an organism, an advanced primate, self-aware, with the gift of anticipation, capable of comprehending his origin and therefore destined to chart his eternal future.

The only enduring value we have gleaned from the world of nature, in the span of all of evolution, is that of survival in an ever wider range of habitation. Life has learned and will continue to learn to endure in an astounding variety of circumstances. But sheer survival, while necessary, is hardly sufficient. It is surely too harsh and too final to be the sole criterion of human value. It is a part of *our* role at this transition point in evolution to be the source of new values in this curious universe.

This is so clearly a heavy responsibility that we try with considerable success to put it off. We have long tried to assume that our values have been given from a higher source. For many, that is such a vital comfort that they dare not question it. Yet for others it is no longer sufficient, and in some sense we have always known that it is man's responsibility to shape his own future.

How shall we approach this ancient burden in this unsteady age? How shall we remold the values of the past, the nostalgic values? The aim of value is the resolution of choice, and the older values seem increasingly inadequate to the newer choices.

I believe science and scientists can indeed contribute to this quest, although I also believe it should not and cannot be their task alone. In truth there are others much more skilled in the arts of synthesis—the artist, the poet, the author, the dramatist, the statesman, the theologian. But the scientist can provide an essential knowledge and a progressive illumination. Our choice of values must depend in part upon our ability to predict their consequences, and hence values must be informed by knowledge. As a corollary we must expect our values to be in part ephemeral. As we know more they must change. The conflict of outmoded values is a prime cause of human tragedy.

There is a sense of endless regression here that has troubled many who think on these matters. We need values. We need values to inform our choice of values, and so on. I am suggesting that to escape this descending spiral we may, and indeed I think we must, seek to orient our values by reference to that holistic universe from which we came and in which we do exist—in sum, to the world of natural science.

I might add that I believe science must for *its* own survival participate in this quest for newer values, for our set of values also determines and measures that which we conceive to be important, and thus it influences that which we choose to abstract and consider from our human experience. Our finite intellects must cope with the experience of an infinite universe and this requires a continual selection based upon relevance, upon importance, upon a sense of value. And it is only within a certain framework of values that we will choose to abstract those discrete but related facts that form the body of science. Our values will determine the resources and the intellect devoted to science and will constrain the approaches science may use.

Scientific knowledge must provide the substructure for the realm of value, and in particular biological knowledge must undergird the values of man. Just as the discoveries of physical science have expanded and refined our perceptions of the external universe, so the discoveries of biological science expand and refine our perceptions of ourselves.

In one sense I conceive the relation of science to value as analogous to, for instance, the relation of chemistry to biology. The processes of biology must accept the constraints of the laws of chemistry. Chemistry can tell us that a given molecular configuration will be unstable or that a given reaction will require a definite input of energy, or that certain chemical processes will be mutually contradictory. And the living cell must work within these boundary conditions. But chemistry cannot determine the function for which the cell may use the given configuration, supply the energy, or, if need be, resolve the contradiction. The integrated cell has, in its organization, resources obedient to, yet greater than, chemical law.

So, too, natural science should be able to define such quantities as the stability of a given social configuration, or the cost (in various coin—psychic, economic, hygienic) of a given action, or even to ascertain the thickets wherein diverse values mutually contradict.

Man's Predicament and Genetic Limitations

Biological science can, I believe, do far more to clarify the issues and perplexities of value. If we can accept the stance that man is the end product of two billion years of the unbroken chain of evolution, that while he is the most remarkable evocation of the power latent in specifically organized matter he is at the same time of a piece with the waves and the particles that comprise the bulk of the universe, then I believe we will see more readily the origins—evolutionary, genetic, physiological—of his characteristic limitations, his anachronisms, his imperfections, and we will, in time, learn to locate and to recognize those internal flaws which underlie his conscious conflicts.

As the science of the biologist continues to penetrate into the redoubt of the mind we shall learn how our very perception of the world is determined by the programs that decompose and reorder our sensory inputs. We shall learn how our actions are spurred or stemmed by the activity of selective centers of motivation and reward, inherited from our remote ancestors. We may even learn to glimpse the limitations imposed upon speech and spatial integration and thought itself by the structures of our brain.

The paradoxes of man—the bleak ironies of the human condition that so compromise our values—are in this view a consequence of his intellectual constraints and his emotional imperatives, of his crude and tentative state as the first sentient animal. We rightly prize truth and we rightly cherish compassion. Yet in the bounded and non-Euclidian world of human value these may sadly diverge—as may love and duty, justice and mercy, individual conscience and collective responsibility, the valued dignity of every man and the indispensable cultivation of excellence.

In this labyrinth of seeming choice and seeming conflict, simple human acts acquire complexity and come to seem multivalued, not merely along the several dimensions of morality but even along each, for specific values are dependent upon past history and future expectation.

Still worse, we must cope with the perturbations of human uncertainty, diffusing and distorting the past and confounding the future. Uncertainty cuts conscience adrift and then sets value in collision with value to paralyze the will and frustrate the heart. Above some critical mass, uncertainty becomes enigma, formless, dimensionless, as impossible to focus as some of the creations of op art. In these enigmas, of which the darkest lie in the mind and character of man, our values wander aimlessly.

The conflicts of morality and the ambiguities of good and evil are in this view akin with the paradoxes of mathematical logic and the ambiguities and illusions in our vision of the ultimate truths of nature.

What we need desperately is biological clarification of the roots and paths of human thought and character and motivation. Very likely we will learn that we are simply not yet equipped to see reality whole and thus we stumble and we wound. We are too new.

Salvation by Amending the Genetic Heritage

If this is so, then the path to the resolution of the human paradox can only be through the genetic breach of our innate limitations. Today even this is conceivable in consequence of the dramatic advances in biological science.

Building upon the profound understanding of the nature of matter achieved by physics and chemistry in the first half of this century, we have in a few decades come to comprehend the material basis of the special organization of life. We have discovered DNA, the agent and the carrier of heredity, the repository of two billion years of evolutionary progress. From this secure and central base we can begin now to mount direct assaults upon the ancient mysteries of development and differentiation and aging, of physiological control, even upon the biology of the mind and the bases of behavior. This knowledge will bring with it the power to intervene—to affect longevity, sex ratio, sibling distribution, perception and intellect, emotion and motivation, pleasure and pain, any human physical or mental characteristic—and thereby to change the very foundations of our social structure.

As if in accord with some cosmic equation as we come better to understand the origins of our dilemmas and our eternal discontent, we shall also come to wield the power to change our inherent nature. Therein will lie choices to challenge all our values. What shall man become?

At that time we will surely have need for a set of values that will not alienate man from his universe, a set of values that may permit man to find his dignity in his unique place at this turning point of evolution which henceforth will be subject to the resources of conscious thought. I believe we should now begin to define such values. In the process we may also very likely illuminate our present dilemmas.

Man has always been doubly tethered to his past—through his genes and through his culture. Until now the cultural tether has been the more elastic. The genetic tether, while undoubtedly changing during the cultural evolution of man, has been the more taut and inflexible. For a very long time we have perforce relied solely upon education as our only means of influencing the human spirit and of improving the condition of man. To point out the difficulty of this project, to suggest the possibility of internal limitations to this process of external cultural manipulation has been rightly enough discouraged as a negative, defeatist approach, for there was no alternative.

Today the hidden part of the iceberg, the biological genetic component of human nature, is coming increasingly into view. Fortunately—perhaps inherently, at the same time—our cultural development has proceeded so far that we can soberly envision the means of remolding these innate patterns, so long submerged and hidden from conscious knowledge. We can foresee the means of making supple our heredity.

Let me say now that we should not expect unlimited elasticity. The patterns of heredity have their own constraints as do those of culture. But in the dynamic interaction of these two modes of change (which has in the past few million years led to man, the creator of culture who is now dependent upon it for his survival and his identity), in this interaction lies the potential for worlds yet undreamed.

Fears Concerning Genetic Technology

I am well aware that there are many who do not regard with optimism this prospect of the designed genetic change of man that I am forecasting. Rather, they find it deeply alarming and repugnant, and for diverse reasons. It is important and instructive to examine these reasons. If it is a comfort to them, this time is not yet upon us. We do not yet have the means; only the possibility now seems very real. To comprehend the human brain and to develop the requisite genetic technology may well require the development of new science equivalent in skill and brilliance and sophistication to the whole of our present science, the product of three centuries of discovery. But that is not a long time in the human experience and I may well overestimate the task.

In part the alarm expressed by many strikes me as an understandable response to profound novelty. We have over the course of time developed a variety of institutions to change and to improve our cultural inheritance—books and the printing press, our educational process (religious and secular), our scientific endeavor. I expect that many of these would have seemed absurd, alien, and even dangerous to a primitive, had someone endeavored to propose a defined program for their development five thousand years ago. These institutions were developed gradually, haltingly, painfully, over the centuries. By simple criteria such as survival they are considered to be advances and have become integral components of our civilization.

Because until now it has simply not been possible, we have not developed institutions to change or improve our biological inheritance. As we now set out to do this no doubt what we may conceive will seem at first absurd, alien, and dangerous. But in the end we may come to see the improvement of our biological inheritance to be as natural and as important as the improvement of our cultural inheritance. Indeed, we might see the two as essential complements, each of the other.

Another voice of alarm is heard from those who believe—with much evidence—that because we are human we should expect to err, and who fear that if we unleash forces beyond human scale, even a minute error may prove to be beyond remedy. This caution we should indeed bear in mind. We must so blend the gifts of foresight and restraint that we do not do that which we cannot undo. The stake here is the entire continuity of evolution. Yet, to quote Alfred North Whitehead, "Panic of error is the death of progress and love of truth is its safeguard."

There are also those who find this entire prospect repugnant, who find a material view of man deeply dehumanizing. I do not really agree. To me it does not devalue man to revalue matter, to appreciate the potential inherent in material organization.

There is a different concern, that if one begins to change the nature of man, he will be, in a profound sense, less human. This could well be. But I cannot celebrate all things human, for there is in us yet too much of our clawing past. Would a man be less human if he never knew hate or rage or envy or terror? Perhaps— in a strange sense he might be less human but more humane.

Would our society be less human if it lacked the crippled, the mentally defective, the emotionally warped or frozen? Perhaps— it would be less varied, less colorful, but also less sordid and harsh, less cruel and pathetic. Men could be less the victims of an ironical fate and more the charters of their individual destinies.

It *is* true that such a man could not comprehend Shakespeare; the Bible would be written in an alien tongue. And it must be our concern that any such changes be gradual, that such persons not feel too rootless, too foreign and remote from all that has gone before, as indeed we do from the other primates.

New Concentrations of Cooperative Action and New Emergents

There are also those who recoil at another prospect; they hear herein the death knell of the doctrine of blame, the dissolution of individual responsibility. To my mind this is hyperbole, but it *is* an overdue recognition of the logical consequence of an increasingly interdependent society.

We are approaching that point in time at which the bonds linking the individual to society, which have become progressively ever firmer, may become stronger than those which sustain his personal integrity, when even his inner nature will have become the consequence of a social decision.

I do not think this need exclude individual responsibility. There is the option that the character of that social decision can yet be such as to strengthen and sustain personal integrity, although we need to recognize and clearly acknowledge this objective.

We must recognize that we are coming to live increasingly in a world of our own design. Unless we choose otherwise, this could be a world in which the unexpected is only a miscalculation and wonder is reserved for the very young—a world in which, as we remold our planet into a projection of our inner selves, we begin to close in upon ourselves—for when all is man-made where shall we gain new inspiration?

The only exit from this cycle will be to change man himself, to escape the tyranny of genetically patterned development, to enlarge his competence, to permit him to acquire new potentials and envision new horizons, to sustain his individual integrity by expanding his capacities to cope with complex and varied circumstances.

I think we do not realize how far we have already proceeded into the bounded, interactive, cooperative society and how this change has exposed the long unresolved questions of value that arise in the tension between the individual and the community. In increasingly crowded and interdependent social organizations —with greatly amplified means of personal expression such as the microphone, the automobile, the rifle—it becomes ever more difficult to act and not interact. We are all joined—economically as interdependent parts of a highly specialized economy, politically and morally as mutually influencing components of our common community, ecologically as jostling residents of a thin layer of a small planet.

For better or worse, we have forged ever stronger social bonds to permit the achievement of specific purpose. We have learned to specialize, to direct and focus the efforts of multitudes of men upon particular goals. The goals can be mean or trivial or they can be great or daring, but the process is the same. We have spawned sophisticated analogues to the more highly adapted specimens of the animal world. The military, armed with weapons of incredible power, encased in armored silos, grows ever more like the dinosaur. The swarming of our youth to Woodstock or Altamont resembles so acutely the swarming of bees to a new field of nectar. Our thoughtless pollution and the rape of our planet remind one of the mindless one-way thrust of the locust horde.

Or alternately, we can wrap man in a cocoon and send him to stir the dust of the moon. We merge our minds to explore the atom and the galaxy, the special architecture of the cell, and the strange circuitry of the brain. Even the progress of art is accelerated through the expanding growth and interaction of the artistic community.

The statistics of cooperativity, the evidence of increased personal cultural interaction, are all about us. In the United States the population density has increased two and a half fold in this century; the pieces of mail per person per year, fourfold; the number of telephone calls per person per year, twentyfold. The statistical-average American drives 4,000 miles per year in an automobile, travels 500 miles per year by airplane, watches television 25 to 30 hours per week. All of these events, all of these actions, increase the number, variety, and range of his social input and output. These numbers are the measures of his cultural bonds.

Many of the new phenomena that so perplex our present society are, I believe, inevitable, if unanticipated, consequences of these increased social interactions abetted by the growth of population density. Confronted by these issues our present values often seem—and are—irrelevant. Here again I believe natural science can help us to comprehend and evaluate these phenomena. Science has long recognized a specific class of processes that critically depend upon circumstances providing a high population density of interacting components.

One of the disturbing features of many current social processes such as, for example, the armaments race or urban decay, is that they appear to be self-propagating. Once initiated and partly grown, they appear to have a life of their own; we seem almost powerless to alter their course. There are similar self-propagating processes in nature that grow critical at a certain size or density. Nuclear reactors, combustion processes, and epidemics are examples of these phenomena, of which the essence is interaction. Each nuclear fission, each molecular reaction, each infection, provides the ingredients for another and another and if the density is high and the boundary conditions do not allow adequate dispersion, then the process is autocatalytic. Such phenomena can of course be controlled, but they must first be understood so that we may *define* the appropriate points of control.

Another feature of our time is the evident impotence of the individual. While our society in a collective sense achieves unprecedented freedoms—from hunger, from disease, from climate—the acceptable range and scope of the individual seems to decrease almost in parallel. At the same time we see increasing discontinuities, abrupt transitions in our social structures and mores. Instead of smooth evolution, we increasingly lurch in unanticipated directions.

Again, we are acquainted with analogous phenomena in natural states dependent upon interactive, cooperative processes. Consider a simple crystal of ice. Once a water molecule is enlisted in such crystal, strongly bonded on all sides, it is no longer free to move about in an autonomous way. If it acquires sufficient energy to depart from its ordered position, it is immediately constrained by its interactions with its neighbors and soon relaxes back into its initial state. Inexorably it rises to the surface of the liquid with its crystal, unable to escape, literally frozen in its course. Only those few molecules at the fringes can through their own energy find release. Elsewhere, only when each molecule in a sufficiently large block acquires an adequate amount of energy at the same time, so that the block can break up en masse, can a real change be effected. Such a circumstance of course is rare and hence change is confined to moments of abrupt transition with correspondingly sharp discontinuities in form and state.

Similarly, in a strongly cooperative society we may expect that change will come to require coordinated action by groups of a size commensurate with the coordinate structure, unless we can deliberately build in some elements to favor autonomy—planes of slippage, hinge points, zones of elasticity—or unless some cataclysmic event thaws the whole structure. In past times war has served as such a cataclysm to disrupt the social order and catalyze new combinations. This social utility is no doubt one of the several factors to account for the viability of war. But now war, always an ugly means, has grown far too destructive for such a purpose.

In no small part the turmoil of our times derives, I believe, from the need, more felt than perceived, to invent new means of thawing our increasingly frozen and unresponsive social order; means of preserving the evident benefits of a cooperative society, yet of adapting it so as to nurture and preserve the dignity of each sentient individual.

Another analogue of a peculiar relevance to a special kind of population density is the action of a laser. Given an inverted population in which a large fraction of the atoms are in a common high energy state, this ensemble can be triggered to yield, autocatalytically, the coherent rapid release of that energy into the intense, narrowly directed beam of the laser. I would suggest an analogy here to an affluent, leisured, human population that can be stimulated into a coherent, rapid release of much of their latent energy into very specific channels. Consider Woodstock or the space program.

But those analogies from science are not just intellectual play, nor are they merely heuristic, for out of cooperative interactive processes new phenomena arise, and what we humans call emergence is born.

As humans we are quite limited in the number of interacting elements that we can hold in our consciousness at one time. It is, then, far more convenient, perhaps imperative, for us to view the outcome of such cooperative interactions as a new quality than always to view it as a complex integral of component qualities.

This is true at so many levels, even, for example, at the level of a benzene molecule. The properties of a benzene molecule may be calculated from the properties of its components, the carbon and hydrogen atoms, strongly interacting in a particular spatial conformation, but it is more often heuristic to discuss the properties of benzene molecules on their own chemical level as distinct qualities. The same is true of the complex interactions that generate the properties of a living cell, of the even more intricate interactive physiology of the human brain, and of the multitude of subtle interactions of our social structure.

And we should, I believe, expect that the newer and tighter modes of reflexive social interaction will in their turn generate what we may best grasp as new and emergent qualities. It seems most likely that man will be living in a dense and cooperative state for some time to come. It is important for us to learn to recognize, by analogy and by observation, the novel characteristics of such a condition. For these more complex situations, the doctrine of emergence becomes an imperative heuristic value for us in consequence of our characteristic limitations.

Antiscientism and Scientists' Responsibility

It would be foolish and discourteous to discuss science and the quest for human values and not to recognize that there are those who believe that science has really no place in such a quest. There is an antiscientism abroad today.

In part this is directed at the asserted hubris of the scientist. To the poet and the philosopher, to the minister and the lawmaker, the scientist with his arcane knowledge and his Faustian technology often seems bound and determined to remold the natural world into a strange and alien creation, shaped in a reflection of man's basic and baser impulses, a sphere wholly pliant to man's lust for control—and many fear an unprecedented peril to a species that would play God.

The scientist is frankly very often bewildered by this charge, so sharply made, of guilt and hubris. I think this cleft of view is important and derives from a fundamental difference in the scale of concern.

The proposals of the scientist are, for him, far from hubris. They are but perturbations in the natural order of things—specialized uses of specialized aggregates of matter. After all, he is not proposing to change the rules of the universe, to invent a new kind of particle, or to repeal the laws of thermodynamics. The scientist lives in a universe whose age is measured in billions of years and whose distances span megaparsecs, in which man is another and very recent life-form in the continuum of ancestral life stretching back with measured and evident change over the tens of hundreds of millions of years. To him it is grossly prideful to propose that evolution should cease with man.

The humanist lives in a world of a very different scale. He is deeply concerned with the much finer distinctions that determine the qualities and gradients of civilization—with the judgment of values and the cultivation of beauty and the refinement of compassion, concepts that first appeared a few thousand years ago and that extend little beyond our planet and our species. Thus to the humanist the proposals of the scientist, which threaten crudely to change the very boundaries and rules of the civilized enterprise, seem grotesque and grossly prideful.

I think there is merit in the continuing debate.

There are other discontents for which I think science is more objectively at fault. The current student thirst for relevance, the intense concern with the environment, is in part a felt recognition of the increasing social interdependence I have mentioned—a search for clues for the means of coping with the problems of a crowded planet and an ever more interactive society. We have, at least in Western culture and Western science, focused overmuch on the discrete object—the molecule, the particle, the gene, the cell. We have undervalued the necessary and inevitable relations of the object with its surroundings—in which and with which and by which it must exist and function. And we see now in part a rejection of the discrete, atomized world of science, which seems to have led us into a midnight of nuclear fission and genetic determinism and existential loneliness on a polluted planet, and a turn to a more holistic view of man, to a sense of place, a sense of man's very special but finite place in nature, a sense of the meaning of each individual's place in society based upon a new understanding of the interaction between genetic and social programming. I believe, as I have indicated, that science has much to contribute to the understanding of these complex environments of man as well as of his internal world. But it has yet done so only scantily.

Also, I believe we have failed miserably in our social algebra. We know the equations of ethics but we utterly neglect their use.

Most of us have learned of the need to equate power with responsibility. Most will agree that knowledge in a technological society is power. How, then, could we assume that we could accumulate great and amoral concentrations of knowledge and wield the immense power thus generated while coasting within the moral guidelines, the low and crumbling retaining walls of mores laid down in an earlier and simpler time? Our secular knowledge has not only far outreached and overshadowed our understanding of morals and ethics, it has inexorably undermined their outmoded social base.

We should have anticipated this. In all human affairs there must be a counterweight. Knowledge, no longer if ever neutral, must be balanced by a concern for its use. We must weld knowledge and concern to maintain our own integrity.

Some have even urged a moratorium in science, an end to the acquisition of knowledge. This, as you might expect, I cannot accept. The only alternative to the quest for knowledge is a vow of eternal ignorance. What an ignoble pledge for the human species—the death of curiosity in the quicksands of fear!

Conclusion

It is true that we have penetrated deeply into the mysteries of matter and of life, and as we near the core of each, the truths we uncover are the more incandescent and by their light we can see to control vast powers. But in truth we are, for all the brilliance of our science and the gleam of our technology, ever immersed in darkness. Outside the flame of human knowledge, slowly expanded with effort and cost, lies the darkness of human ignorance, both without and within. We know not yet where we are or what we are. And the human effort—the effort of this fragile, so recent product of evolution—to ask and answer these questions has been, is, and will be our meaning and our purpose.

In a time of dismay, in an age almost severed from the past, it is natural to seek comfort in a yet unscarred future. We hope, with very human and touching hope, somehow to elude the dark foreshadow of causality, for of course the seeds of the future are already sown.

We are, it seems to me, in consequence of our long and gradual evolution, inevitably a flawed and limited and imperfect creature, with a saving grace, a slight margin, a slight imbalance toward a higher life. And what we must seek to do—by every means— is to amplify that imbalance, to widen that margin, to enlarge the humane and diminish the bestial.

Historians tell us that all previous civilizations have flourished for a time and have then declined. In a real sense they have been the victims of their success, which has bred rigidity of cultural pattern, indolence born of relative affluence, and the luxury of repeated warfare. If we are to avoid a similar fate, we must not devote our resources to similar folly—toward which we are well on the road. Rather, we must deliberately invest in the enterprises of self-renewal—in education and health, which generation by generation improve our culture; in the continuous acquisition of new knowledge of nature and of man; and now, for the first time, in the very novel possibility of the gradual improvement of our genetic base—in the enhancement of the inheritance of the race.

We have always relied upon a few individuals, rarely gifted, at the outer limits of human capability to lead us out of the brute past. In science we discovered a magnificent tool to corroborate and cumulate the efforts of these few over many generations. They have led the rest of us out of darkness by example and persuasion and promise. It has been, in a deep sense, a thin margin.

Now we may reasonably soon achieve something new. We may increase the number of those who can so lead and we may increase the adaptability of all to follow into a higher plane.

We need to do so, for an unanticipated and perilous by-product of our progress has been the growing fracture of our culture. As we increase knowledge and refinement in every field of endeavor the time and effort required to master each discipline has grown to divide us into distinct, noncommunicating, cultural species. To reintegrate men we need to enhance, genetically, our capacities relative to our opportunities, to augment the ability of each to comprehend the other.

In so doing, however, I hope we will always bear in mind the distinctive value of our individual humanity. A living cell maintains its integrity only because every component is constrained by its structure and disposition to interact specifically and exclusively with those other components with which it should interact. There can be no molecular anarchy.

An insect society functions in an analogous manner. With only half a million neurons per individual, the insect has achieved efficiency and survival—and evolutionary stagnation—through total specialization. With ten billion neurons per individual, *we* should be able to create a very different, a far more flexible, means for social advantage. As human beings we should aim to create a new mode of cooperative organization, one in which anarchic interaction is restricted not by rigid inherited structure and stereotyped response but by conscious understanding, by anticipation, by wisdom and grace and compassion—a social order that seeks to maintain and to augment its capacity for creative innovation tempered by simple humanity.

The aims of genetic technology should be to enhance the capacities of each individual to comprehend and to cope freely with the complexities of interactive society, to enlarge the internal margin of humanity, to transcend our conceptual limitations. I would offer five maxims for the future genetic technology; they are couched in borrowed terms:

Do not eliminate all of chance and novelty—for that is the way to extinction. Do not create defined subtypes—for that is the way of the ant. Do not chill all passion—for that is the way of the drone. Do not diminish the heart—for that is the way of the robot. And do not erase the ego—for that is the way of the slave.

Paul Tillich wrote, "Man becomes truly human only at the moment of decision." We should aim always to enlarge his opportunities and capacities for decision.

I have hoped to show that science can and must contribute to the quest for human values. In essence, the answer to our quest is to be found in the ancient injunction, "Know thyself." We are only beginning to perceive the depth and the danger of that task.

We cannot know the end of this voyage—whether there is some Elysium wherein serenity replaces paradox and the good and the evil are forever uncoupled or whether there is an inherent tension between the domain of will and sentience and the inscrutable universe in which we so strangely arise. That is left for the future and the future's future.

CHAPTER VII

A Scientific View
of the Role of Religion

Ralph Wendell Burhoe

Reflections on the Relevance
of Religion for Human Values

Before looking at the nature of religion and its relevance for
human values, I would like to comment on some notions about
the relevance of religion as reflected in the previous six chapters.

In Chapter I it was suggested that values arise out of the memories of norms or standards that indicate what it is necessary or
good to do to maintain and advance a living system. It was there
held that values are norms or standards necessary for the state of
life that must be maintained in an environment continually
threatening to disrupt it. Hence in living systems, values are
linked with various means of detecting the present trends and of
anticipating or prophesying future states of self and environment,
so as to be informed as to what to do to maintain the norms
necessary for life. Furthermore this system of goals and information (anticipating what future conditions will be) is tied in all
living systems to a means for adapting to those conditions, so
as to maintain life's norms (homeostasis) in spite of changed
conditions.

In Chapter II we considered briefly some of the promises and
threats prophesied on the basis of technological trends for the
coming millennium. We also reviewed some of the gloomy

auguries for religion and human values. It was suggested that the radical changes of the current cultural revolution that is sweeping the world were not only disrupting the effectiveness of traditional religious and value systems but were also offering the possibility of the greatest religious reformation of, perhaps, the last hundred thousand years.

In Chapter III we found further evidence that technology is transforming the human value situation, but it was suggested that the newer views of the nature of reality coming out of the same sciences that produce technology give us a new understanding of reality as a matter of relationships rather than of substances. It was suggested that man is fully a part of this reality, that the reality is evolving and hence man is evolving, and that while the changes carry threats as well as potentials, we should not be dominated by fear. Physicist Schilling finds the Christian tradition still very relevant for moving ahead safely into vast technological changes. His hopeful conclusion is based on man's goals being in accord with those of God.

Chapter IV suggested that while we can be grateful for new technological comforts, the salvation myths coming out of the sciences and technology were at least as ambiguous and even less empirical than those of the Biblical religious myths. Theologian Gilkey suggests that logically man cannot be at one and the same time the mechanically determined product of objective scientific laws and also be the free carver of his own fate as some scientific utopias suggest. Like physicist Schilling, he feels that man's ground for hope rests in God. But Gilkey's formulation of the God concept seems more explicitly critical. For him, God is an intuited, cosmic, ontological ground of hope, or an ultimate order or scheme in history and social process, developed, as in most human schemes of meaning, to balance the more realistic view of man.

But in Chapters V and VI we do not find prophecies of the continued value of the Christian tradition. In Chapter V, psychologist Mowrer looks at the problem of values (good and evil) in the light of his psychology and related sciences to show how social values are related to or involved in psychological and social adjustment. He dismisses the religious myths or symbols of values that are dependent on a metaphysical or theistic ground, but he suggests that a "church" of the future will for psychosocial reasons be found necessary for seeking the good and avoiding the evil, and will exist in groups of mutual human support, including especially small "house churches." Even though long-range hedonistic self-interest will motivate men to espouse good and shun evil, they need the information and force of a group, of a cultural tradition, to guide them. It can be noted that he envisions, as I do, a religious reformation far more extensive than that of the sixteenth century. Mowrer's salvation is dependent on cultural reformation or evolution.

In Chapter VI, biophysicist Sinsheimer expresses fear that cultural evolution may not be sufficient to meet the value requirements of the future, because man's ancient biological heritage may not be adequate to provide him with the higher level of understanding and social responsibility that will be required in a huge, dense, interacting population. He therefore suggests that technologically we can, and perhaps for survival and entry into the new age we must, improve our genetic heritage: that is, design more capable and more benign human biological bases. Like Schilling, Sinsheimer sees as one of our greatest needs the finding of ways by which a huge, interacting, global population can act sufficiently responsibly and cooperatively to make life possible under the technology that brings all the world together in one interdependent whole. For him, as for Mowrer, the sciences are seemingly a currently more useful source and guide in the quest for values in the coming age than are the religious myths, Biblical or otherwise.

This book on values in the new millennium was commissioned by a theological school celebrating its 175th anniversary. Presumably it was hoped that the book might provide some vision for the future of the school and for the future of religious institutions in general. Human values must have been presumed to be related to churches and their ministry. But, a review of the book may leave us with mixed feelings and doubts rather than clarification of the role of religion in human values. On the one hand, the grand religious reformations prophesied by Mowrer or myself might not be recognized as properly *religious* by many. On the other hand, traditional religion may have lost its power. See the "predictions concerning religion" in Chapter II. Gilkey declares that "God talk" is essential, but then says in Chapter IV that "a transcendent, ultimate, sacred dimension or factor is [because of scientific culture] thus unreal to us"; it seems superstitious and unreal, like shades that vanish in the light of day. Two of the scientists in this book fail to draw seriously on God concepts. Hence we can wonder if the traditional religions and their notions are perhaps irrelevant for values in the third millennium A.D.

But I reject any conclusion that the sciences today make God talk either incredible or irrelevant. I feel that Gilkey is quite right in saying science raises the ultimate question of human hope more poignantly than ever. However, although I join him in affirming that "the confidence for the future even of technological man can only be grounded if the coming work of the Lord in the affairs of men is known and affirmed," I find myself forced to reject his dismissal of the sciences from theology. For it is from the sciences that I get my answers for questions about human hope, my understanding of cosmic reality on which human destiny depends, and my knowledge and affirmation of the "work of the Lord in the affairs of men."

I hope that in the remainder of this book I can show that each of the four other authors is making a valid and indispensable contribution to our understanding of human values and religion in the future, even though there seems to be, at least on the surface, some grave differences. But first we should attempt a fuller view of the nature and function of religion.

The Nature and Function of Religion as Seen from Scientific Perspectives

The split of modern cultures between the new sciences and technologies on the one hand and traditional religions and philosophies of human values on the other is what is bringing us to a crisis of technology and values in this century. It is the healing of this split by a new synthesis, a new emergent in cultural evolution, that I prophesy as not only possible but as already on the way. The synthesis requires the full and honest use of the essential elements of both sides of the split. To begin with, my account must attempt to provide a better and more modern understanding of the nature or function of religion itself and its role in values and its historical and potential future integrations with the sciences. To give this "deeper" and more viable understanding of the role of religion, I draw on the very scientific world view that is said to be so dangerous and lethal for religion. While this may seem like going to the enemy for aid, I shall draw on the sciences to help understand what religions are all about.

This attempt to express in the language of the scientific world view what is the nature of religion should harm religion no more than the attempt to understand medical problems in modern scientific language harms medical practice. If the evil spirits bothering some psychotics are found to be unintegrated early memory traces, or genetic or chemical errors, no one is going to object if this new understanding helps to cure the patient. I do not mean by this to suggest that either psychiatric or religious problems are usually this simple. But I am suggesting that there is nothing to prevent success in scientific investigation of very complex problems, even the problems of man's mind and his ultimate hopes and values, his religions. To begin this we need to know more clearly in scientific language just what we can credibly and usefully mean by the term "religion." At the same time, I trust that this definition will remain faithful to the basic truths and realities still inherent in the great religious traditions.

In Chapter I, it was noted that life is today understood by many scientists as an "open system" that remains stable in spite of disrupting influences because it is regulated or controlled by an integrated network of cybernetic subsystems that anticipate the disrupting influences and by negative feedback keep the total life system stable or alive. Life as an open system achieves stability (or what the philosophers and theologians would call "being") by means of very complexly regulated dynamic operations. As Schilling suggests, even physical "being" is active interaction. Life systems or living beings are also dynamic patterns of interaction. I also indicated that life systems are made up of complexly inter-related subsystems and supersystems of various levels. Man in the scientific world view is made up from subsystems of organs, which are made up of cells, which are made up of molecules; and at the same time he is made up of elements fed to him from the levels of supersystems: he is structured by inputs from his family, his local society, from the total species, and ultimately from the ecosystem of the world and the cosmos.[1]

Now, living systems at every level must be regulated or struc-tured or maintained in their characteristic and necessary order by some kinds of controls that produce the characteristic dynamic order. This applies to societies as well as to individual men. Some-times the controls (cybernetic systems) that regulate the satis-faction of the requirements for both the individual and the society are housed in the same controlling station. For instance, in social insects the control for fulfilling both individual and social needs is largely housed in the genotypes, the genetic code that structures each individual.[2] Of course, human societies are not structured very specifically by the human genotype but rather by culture or culture types.[3]

Along with a number of anthropologists and others, I use the term "religion" to designate the cultural core of the information by which the basic social values and behaviors are structured and are related to the individual human values and behaviors. This is a description of the nature of religion. The religious aspects of the human culture type in large part do for human social and personal values what the genotype does for social insects: they provide the information that organizes or controls man's sense of good and evil in a way that integrates his personal needs with his social needs.

It is significant to note that, without the cultural transmission of social values, men do feel, sense, and behave well with respect to a large number of private, individual, organic values, goals, needs, or desires. But without the cultural transmission of the social values they have very little in the way of well-structured and viable social motivations and behaviors above the level of the nuclear family. Thus the evolution of the various types of human societal structures and values is not significantly registered in the human genotype but primarily in its culture types. You are not born with a native language or with native manners, morals, or understanding of the world and your role in it. By looking carefully at the phenomena usually designated by the term "religion," one seems justified to conclude that the more central, fundamental, or ultimate values of society (and individual, too) are registered in and structured by the religious elements of the culture. One might then properly say, in systems-theory language, that religions are the top of the hierarchy of the integrated net of cybernetic mechanisms that shape human social behavior and integrate the social and personal needs of men. The original title of Mowrer's chapter was "The Problem of Good and Evil Empirically Considered with Reference to Psychological and Social Adjustment." He well understands how the religious institution is basic for integrating man's personal and social needs.

One can also say that religions are the agencies in which is registered the cumulated information that regulates the dynamic life patterns that integrate personal and social values. That is, religion represents the tradition or body of information that structures the values that make human social life or civilization possible. This is properly called a sacred tradition. When the integrating of personal and social values fails in a society, the society dies. Police and armies cannot hold together in orderly behavior a population that has lost its convictions as to why it makes sense to serve the moral requirements or traditional notions of the society as to what is good and necessary. This is especially true when these moral requirements seem to deny the gratification of men's inner organic needs and values. The society under such conditions may crack up internally, and be destroyed from the disorderly conduct of the individuals who make it up. As I pointed out earlier, death and disorder are closely related. The inefficacy of religion in a society is akin to the inefficacy of the genotype in an ant society. If there are mutations that render a certain species of ants unable to cooperate socially to meet their combined social and individual needs, as in their past tradition, all the offspring of that mutated genotype perish. Human societies are informed or dynamically structured by their cultures, and without culture Homo sapiens is not viable.

In our account of cybernetic or order-maintaining systems, I indicated that in addition to the established information as to what are the values or goals of the system, there has to be an instrument to see that the goals are in fact reached, that the values are attained. Religions, as cybernetic mechanisms that provide the dynamic structures of integrated basic human personal and social values, must involve not only the "information" about values (this is related to myths, sacred texts, and theologies), but it must also involve the mechanisms or motivations for attaining these goals. This means that the myths and other patterns of information must be transmitted so that the values or norms are established inside the central nervous systems of the individuals who make up the society so that they are motivated to achieve the values and goals. This is related to religious rites and acts. In the first function above, as a storehouse and communicator of information, religion functions as do the other societal sources of knowledge, including the sciences and educational institutions. In the second function, the transmission and evocation of the characteristic attitudes and behavioral patterns of a culture, religion operates as what we commonly call an art or technology.

Among the primitive arts or technologies of our ancestors, along with the making and using of weapons and other tools of stone and bone and wood, along with skin clothes and shelters, and perhaps as early as the earliest fire technology a half million years ago, there arose among men this very special art or technology of religion. Religion was thus a part of man's evolving cultural adaptations to the reality in which he lived and moved and had his being. We do not have any better or fuller data on origins of religion in genus *Homo* than we do on those of many of his other arts or technologies, but scientific studies are providing new ways of conceiving religion that greatly extend our earlier notions, which were limited to our parochial traditions and the associated artifacts, including sacred books. To the earlier tools for investigating religious phenomena by linguists, archaeologists, historians, and others, there have been added carbon-14 dating of sacred scrolls, computer analysis of linguistic expressions, and other techniques based on modern science. These are all building up a new vision and context for understanding religion.

But the very nature of our understanding of religion is being transformed by the scientifically enlarged vision of the nature of man and history of life entirely apart from any studies of religions as such. Newly established theories from many scientific disciplines are enabling us to view religion from a new perspective. Just as recent work has fitted the Biblical symbols of Adam and Eve (whom Bishop Ussher estimated to have flourished some six thousand years ago) into the larger context of a few thousand thousand years of cultural evolution, and fit the Biblical story of the creation of earlier living systems of plants and animals into the few thousand thousand thousand years of organic evolution, so must we transform our total understanding of the nature of religion and of the place of our parochial, Western, recent, Judeo-Christian tradition into the scheme of cosmic history. While a child or a man who has never before heard of a foreign language may on his first exposure laugh and wonder why the speaker is making such queer noises or nonsense, the sophisticated linguist may find each new piece of linguistic evidence a fascinating piece in a grand picture puzzle of the marvelous forms and the history of languages. If we add to that the new information and theories from comparative physiology and communication theory and natural selection in cultural evolution, we get a significant new perspective on the evolution of language where our rational understanding may be suffused with wonder, awe, and aesthetic marvel. I suggest that similar developments are under way in our developing understanding of religion over the past century. I shall give below new ways in which the nature of religion may be reconceived even within the theoretic concepts of physics as well as of the biological and psychosocial sciences.

Religions may today be seen as an integral part of the total spectrum of cosmic history, as a particular section made by the nature of events in human cultural evolution on earth. In a larger context we can begin to see what religions are for, what they do, how they serve man, how they are, indeed, a gift of "super-human" powers that select the adaptations of men and their societies to their particular ecological niches, psychosocial as well as geographic. It is a remarkable twist of history that a century after Darwin it is some of the scientists rather than the theologians who are providing the most powerful and most constructive rational defenses of religion and a sense of its cosmic relevance.

For instance, an agnostic psychologist at Northwestern University (to whose paper on cultural evolution I have already referred) has said with a good deal of puckishness on several occasions that when he has been talking to theologians and clergymen he is surprised to find that he, on scientific grounds, has more respect for traditional religion than they, the professional apologists for religion, do. He has written: "I will argue on evolutionary grounds that it is just as rational to follow well winnowed religious traditions which one does not understand as it is rational to continue breathing air before one understands the role of oxygen in bodily metabolism. I will argue that if modern psychology and social science disagree with religious tradition on ways of living, one should, on rational and scientific [apart from any religious] grounds, choose the traditional [religious] recipes for life, for these are the better tested. . . . I will argue as did Pascal, but on evolutionary grounds, that 'the heart has its reasons which Reason does not understand,' and that it is *rational* to follow an evolved heart in such matters."[4] It is indeed ironic that at the same time as a scientist is thus suggesting the "wisdom of religious culture" on grounds similar to that of biological scientists who have marveled at the "wisdom of the body"[5] cumulated in preconscious evolution, other social scientists as well as internal analysts of the religious community are finding, as we saw in Chapter II, that inside the religious institutions and theological schools there is increasing loss of faith in the relevance and meaningfulness of their religious language and theology.

In 1961, Anthony F. C. Wallace, who is now head of the department of anthropology at the University of Pennsylvania, presented a paper on "Religious Revitalization" in which he outlined the essence of the religious process that ties it to the basic characteristic of life: organization.

In view of the near-universality of religion among men, its antiquity, and the multiple functions which it seems to serve, it would seem that we may speak of "the religious process" as a type of event which occurs among human beings under very widely varying conditions. The essential theme of the religious event is, nevertheless, definable: it is the dialectic of disorganization and organization. On the one hand men universally observe the increase of entropy (disorganization) in familiar systems: metals rust and corrode, woods and fabrics rot, people sicken and die, personalities disintegrate, social groups splinter and disband. And on the other hand, men universally experience the contrary process of organization: much energy is spent preventing rust, corrosion, decay, rot, sickness, death, and dissolution, and indeed, at least locally, there may be an absolute gain of organization, a real growth or revitalization. This dialectic, the "struggle" (to use an easy metaphor) between entropy and organization, is what religion is all about. The most diverse creeds unite in the attempt to solve the sphinx-riddle of the relationship between life and death, between organization and disorganization; the ideas of the soul, of gods, of world cycles, of Nirvana, of spiritual salvation and rebirth, of progress—all are formal solutions to this problem, which is indeed felt intimately by all men.

But religion does not offer just any solution: it characteristically offers a solution which assures the believer that life and organization will win, that death and disorganization will lose, in their struggle to become the characteristic condition of self and cosmos. And religion further attempts to elucidate and describe the organization of self and cosmos. Religion then may be said to be a process of maximizing the quantity of organization in the matrix of perceived human experience. Religion maximizes it, perhaps, beyond what rational use of the data of this experience would justify, but it thereby satisfies a primary drive. We must, I think, postulate an organization "instinct": an "instinct" to increase the organization of cognitive perception. Religion and science, from this point of view, would seem to be the more direct expressions of this organizational instinct.[6]

Here is a classic statement about the nature of religion. It is a statement that comes out of a significant scientific study of religions, not just Christianity, but all kinds of the more than one hundred thousand different species of religions he has estimated to have flourished among men during the past one hundred thousand years of man's history. And it shows on both the empirical and the theoretical grounds of the sciences that religion's function lies in the control center of living systems, providing homeostasis, maintaining or producing organization, producing viability. It shows religion as a central organizer of perceived human experience. It also shows religion in its cosmic setting, as a part of the ongoing process that has been establishing on earth higher levels of information and organization for several billion years, long before our present mountains were brought forth. I find such a description of religion from the perspective of the scientific world view a more credible apology to the "secular" or "scientific" mind for the relevance and reality of religion and its eternal truth and function than one could find from many or most internal or parochial apologists of the separate religions. As a central part of the always necessary organization for maintaining and generating functions of life, religion is universal.

Of course, I recognize that some theologians claim there is no "religion in general," nothing about them that is universal or that can be generalized. But such assertions I am forced to set aside as both unscientific and historically parochial. For, just as it is necessary to interpret and make religion credible to a secular and scientific culture, it is also necessary to do the same with respect to other religious cultures. Paul and other church fathers knew how to speak to the religion and culture of Athens. Anyway, from a rational and scientific analysis of the function of religions—that of providing people with the beliefs necessary for their hopeful and courageous orientation toward organization and order in the midst of seemingly chaotic and discouraging circumstances—it would seem that religion is perennial and, in this abstract sense, invariant, so long as there is any human culture.

But an anthropologist is not the only one to suggest a connection between religion and the physical law of entropy. Let me introduce you to a physicist who, I believe, never heard of anthropologist Wallace or his theory connecting religion with thermodynamics and entropy. What I am trying to emphasize by saying this is that a reality or truth intrinsic to the nature of things will lead scientists to common notions, even though they start from different scientific cultures and may never have heard of one another. R. B. Lindsay, of Brown University, in his book *The Role of Science in Civilization*[7] points out that the second law of thermodynamics may be interpreted as the tendency in any naturally occurring process for systems to proceed from order (Wallace's "organization") to disorder or to randomness. Yet systems of increasing order do occur locally, which are paid for by decreased order elsewhere, and the most striking cases are living organisms. He says: "The production of a living creature on no matter how humble a level is a vivid example of the transformation of disorder into order. From a random collection of atoms of oxygen, nitrogen, hydrogen, and carbon, with a few others thrown in, are synthesized the remarkably elaborate chemical constituents of the living cell, and these cells in turn arrange themselves functionally in intricate but orderly fashion," to fashion, we could add, animals, men, human behavior, human culture, and religions. From the point of view of ordinary physical processes in closed systems, the development and maintenance of living systems (including religions) is highly improbable, but understood as open systems operating under natural selection over time, they are today being said by many scientists to be inevitable.[8]

The same is true not only for the development and maintenance of cells and organisms but also with regard to the behavior of men. Lindsay points out that "the development of civilization itself may be in a certain sense looked upon as the result of the attempt of man to introduce order into his environment." Houses are more than piles of stones. Communication of information by language similarly is not just noise. A message is an imposition of order on disorder. Information, organic life, and human culture are all found to be kindred phenomena, characterized by their degree of orderliness that is highly improbable, certainly improbable in terms of ordinary physics, describing systems containing no highly structured boundary conditions. Life, including human culture, tends in just the opposite direction from what the second law of thermodynamics says is probable for any closed system.

However, neither Lindsay nor any of the other competent physicists who have investigated this problem suppose that the second law of thermodynamics is violated by this tendency of life to move in a direction which is the reverse of that followed by the rest of its environment. In fact, they all point out that life's increasing order is paid for by an equal or greater decrease of order elsewhere in the system.

But it is just this common and universal characteristic of life— its characteristic high degree of order or organization—that helps us to understand and define something very essential about the nature of life in contrast to what is nonliving. Here, in one of the most basic laws of physics, the second law of thermodynamics, we are finding a definition of life and life's function that is opening a window for understanding ourselves and our relation to the cosmos around us in a rich new way. This window was opened by such famous physicists and mathematicians as Erwin Schrödinger (1945)[9] and Norbert Wiener (1948)[10] only a couple of decades ago. It opens a window of light to illuminate the heart of life's values, an objective criterion that may be capable of guiding man in all his future developments.

Lindsay points out that life, viewed as an "entropy-consuming" or order-building program "contains a powerful suggestion that man as a creature with a highly developed nervous system has an obligation to act deliberately as an entropy consumer to put himself in tune with the very principle of life which he and his existence represent." He notes, however, that sometimes, instead of creating order, men are

arsonists and murderers, the former destroying by fire what was carefully and slowly constructed by human labour and thus producing a vast increase in entropy in a short time, and the latter reducing in an instant the highly complicated but very orderly arrangement of molecular constituents we call a human individual to the equivalent of a heap of disorderly rubble with a similar enormous relative increase in entropy. We call such people criminals and enemies of society, precisely because they sin against the aim of man to produce and maintain order in his affairs. On a less tragic scale it is not without significance that we attach the word disorderly to the alcoholic and the drunkard. They are nuisances to society in that they produce more than their fair share of the disorder in a social milieu which strives for entropy consumption. . . . Even the thoughtless litterbug who strews the landscape with his rubbish is in his lowly way an unnecessary entropy producer.

But in spite of these melancholy examples, man in his better moments seems to exemplify a ceaseless urge to force some order on his experience. The very existence of science is an example of this. This reflects a conscious desire and involves thoughtful planning limited, to be sure, to a certain small fraction of the population but implying consequences for all mankind. . . .

Considerations of this kind seem to suggest a new kind of imperative which if reasonably interpreted might serve as a satisfactory basis for an ethical code. We shall call it the *thermodynamic imperative* and phrase it as follows: All men should fight always as vigorously as possible to increase the degree of order in their environment, i.e., consume as much entropy as possible, in order to combat the natural tendency for entropy to increase and for order in the universe to be transformed into disorder, in accordance with the second law of thermodynamics.[11]

The definition of life in terms of cosmic laws and conditions has been considerably advanced and refined since the above-mentioned writings of Schrödinger, Wiener, Wallace, Lindsay, and many other scientists of various kinds during the period of some ten to twenty years ago. Recently I have been impressed by the work of J. Bronowski, Aharon Katchalsky, and others.[12] In the light of more recent findings, some of the earlier formulations, such as Lindsay's "thermodynamic imperative," require some refinements. But the new developments on the whole seem to increase rather than decrease the meaningful relationship of man and human values to the nature and lawful operations of the cosmos. These developments promise grounds for understanding human values objectively and grounds for illuminating the religious or sacred elements of human destiny.

Bronowski in the article cited above[12] provided a theoretical model that explains the continuity and sequence of evolution from atoms to cells and higher living systems as a *necessary* result of the interaction of the characteristic randomizing tendencies revealed in thermodynamics with the potential structures or "preferred configurations and hidden stabilities" which are empirically given or found to characterize the nature of the cosmos as a hierarchy of successive layers or strata of stability. "Because stability is stratified," he says, "evolution is open, and *necessarily* [here the italics are mine] creates more and more complex forms. There is therefore a peculiar irony in the vitalist claim that the *progress of evolution from simple to complex* cannot be the work of chance. On the contrary, as we see, exactly this *is how chance works, and is constrained to work by its nature.* . . . So long as there remains a potential of stability which has not become actual, there is no other way for chance to go."

Bronowski's model explains why Lindsay's and Wallace's ethical and religious imperatives to search for and maintain ever higher systems of order are in fact what they are by the very nature of the universe. His model also explains the relation of these successive levels of order and stages of evolution to the second law of thermodynamics. By means of the hierarchy of preferred configurations or stable states on the way to equilibrium, he accounts for what Lindsay and others have called the negentropic direction of evolving systems of life, and his model shows in sharper detail how this direction is related to the negentropy defined in classical thermodynamics, which deals with closed systems in which there is no hierarchy of preferred configurations or stable states.

Katchalsky, working in non-equilibrium thermodynamics and flow phenomena, also finds life derived as a natural product of the world described by physicists, that "life is not an improbable event, but the product of great cosmic phenomena which could convert inorganized matter into well-developed patterns."[12] These and many similar descriptions of the origin and characteristics of life and life's trends, goals, and destiny in the context of the nature of the cosmos and cosmic laws also help us to understand, using the same general scientific model or scheme of things, how life and life's values are related to the cybernetic and negative-feedback mechanisms of man's engineering devices, to the related homeostatic mechanisms of living systems described by biologists, and to the psychosocial scientist's descriptions of the cybernetic or control mechanisms that regulate psychological and social behavior and feeling and thinking, or become human values.

In a tour of the levels of organization and stability from atoms through cells, organisms, and societies, our descriptions are continually required to include a hierarchy of levels of systems of the natural world around us, which in their larger patterns are called ecosystems and which at any level may be called the environment of the entity we are contemplating. Living systems at all levels from cells to human societies are seen as inextricably interwoven with and dependent on the environing strata of ecosystems. We find a fascinating panorama of man's at-oneness with the cosmos, with the total scheme of things. And we can describe the origins and the grounds for more and more of our existing values from the health of our bodies to the health of our souls, our societies, and our ecosystem. We can even describe imperatives about what to do when we do not yet have clearly defined values internalized in us concerning certain areas of our encounters.

Significant for religion is the growing body of leading scientists in all disciplines from mathematical physics through the biological sciences to the human psychosocial sciences who are finding a common perspective that defines all living systems at all levels of their structure and that defines their goals or functions within the total scheme of things. This perspective goal is universal and applicable to every time and place, to every society, person, animal, plant, and microbe. Here is a sharper, clearer, more comprehensive definition and understanding of the nature of human values by the light of the sciences than any religion, theology, or philosophy has hitherto produced.

One must note that these scientific approaches are pointing not only to what we ordinarily call mundane human values, but are giving a sharper definition of the more fundamental or supremely significant religious values and are finding an invariant characteristic of the nature of living systems in the cosmos from which our whole hierarchy of values, including each unique individual's values at this moment, can, in principle at least, be logically inferred. I cannot imagine a more important bonanza for theologians and the future of religion than the information lode revealed by the scientific community. It provides us with a clear connection between human values, including our highest religious values, and the cosmic scheme of things. While it is true that some scientific concepts are inimical to some particular religious formulations, especially at primitive levels of analysis, what is becoming clear is that when one discusses the basic features of religious function in terms of the developing universal symbols or language of the sciences, then the phenomena and the truths of human values and religions may be considered not as vanishing mists of superstitions in the new morning of the scientifically illluminated day of human understanding, but as an integral part of the scientific scheme of things.

In the light of these facts, it seems to me inevitable that religion will be flourishing in the twenty-first century even more effectively than at the present moment when we are still experiencing the breaking up of patterns of culture and the reshuffling of the codes of information that are obsolete within the newly emerging context of human life. I share with Jaspers and Henry Nelson Wieman the feeling that we are on the threshold of the greatest religious reformation in twenty-five hundred years. I suggest that these contributions from scientists tell us something of the shape of the new patterns of religious order that will provide men with their sense of meaning and duty in the new age.

The Queen Is Dead—Long Live the Queen

In order to accent a historically unique feature of the religious reformation or revolution at the dawn of the third millennium, I wish to point more clearly at what I have been from time to time only hinting when I have suggested that religion is an art or technology.

I shall start by comparing the salvatory arts of medicine and religion. No one will quarrel with the statement that the two human arts of healing called medicine and religion have had an intertwined history. Most everyone knows that in primitive societies the shaman was priest and medicine man in one; and many today understand the closeness of function of the counseling religious pastor and psychotherapist. We should remember also that both medicine and religion are concerned with the same program of enhancing the homeostasis, the order, the organization, or healthiness of life. The difference between them seems to be that the art of medicine has specialized more at the levels of general organismic function while the art of religion has specialized more on the organization of man's social roles and his consequent attitudes toward himself, his fellowmen, and his place in the world. This soul-healing function of religion keeps it still close to that branch of medicine called psychotherapy or psychiatry, since that is an art that is concerned with the management of man's attitudes as they are structured in his central nervous system and are manifested in his behavior. But, until very recently anyway, psychiatry has been more involved with the individual, and not so much with useful doctrines or applications that contribute to the enhancement of order, organization, or homeostasis of a society of individuals, or the therapy of sick societies. Still less have the psychiatric sciences contributed to the art of ordering the attitudes of the individual (or the society) with respect to any objective reality transcendent to himself and to his society. The art of medicine is clearly distinguishable from the art of religion.

But, because it is of the essence for understanding the potential future of religion, I want to go beyond the above comparison of the close relationship of medicine and religion to make two points. I want to suggest that I could have used with equal propriety the term "technology" as well as "art" to describe or name either medicine or religion. Even though in our language the word "art" by itself has come commonly to stand for what is more properly designated as "fine art," the only basic difference between art and technology is that "art" is from the Latin and "techne" is from the Greek, meaning about the same thing: the systematic application of knowledge or skill in effecting a desired result or practical purpose. Now, my two points.

First is that I was asked to comment on trends in technology and their implications for human values, and my survey of the arts and technologies and their trends leads me to prophesy that the one technology with by far the most significance for human values at the end of the second millennium is religion. All the other technologies—including the scientific-miracle technologies of space travel, atomic energy, computers, even medicine—are trivial for human values compared with religion. Religion, if you follow what Wallace was saying about it, is the very center of man's most advanced evolutionary thrust to find order or organization, governing his overall attitudes and behaviors with respect not only to himself and his fellowmen but also with regard to the ultimate realities of that cosmos in which he lives and moves and has his being. This view of religion would make it the central cultural agency incarnating, in Lindsay's language, the thermodynamic imperative—a key for our understanding of life and its further development.

A second point is that the great reformation of world religion, which others and I are prophesying for the period when the second millennium turns into the third, will arise like the recent reformations in the medical arts from scientific sources. I am suggesting that religion will follow medicine, perhaps a century or two behind, in finding the radically new scientific revelations or myths of the nature of man and his world fruitful for its mythology. I am suggesting that the art of religion, like the art of medicine, will become an applied science.

By this, I do not mean that religion in the past failed to be intelligent, or that it was without rational wisdom. I have already suggested that religious myths were attempts at explanatory hypotheses that were as early as those of any realm of human culture. But, it is clear that religion in the West has largely been handicapped by its expression in terms of the myth or science of the Greco-Roman world, and on similarly ancient systems of conceiving man and his world for the religions of mankind. This is not to despise the science of the axial period of Jaspers, of some twenty-five hundred years ago. For its time in each culture it was as good a science as our present one. Probably the sacredness, the ultimate importance, of religious doctrine has been a factor tending to the preservation of its statements in the language or symbols of the Greco-Roman world view. Religions are properly conservative. There are many other factors in the slowness of religions to reform their myths to conform to the evolving myths of the sciences of the past century. I will not attempt to set them forth here.

What is important to note is that the time has come and now is when religious doctrine must be revised to accord with that of the contemporary images that men hold credible about the nature of the world and of themselves. I have pointed to the trends in American religion for adopting psychotherapeutic practices, even though the myths of religion and psychiatry have never been very successfully integrated. We could also contemplate the amazing mission of the Marxist myth based on nineteenth-century social theory. This eschatology and prophecy of a redeemed mankind through sacrificial struggle to conform to the necessities believed to be called for by history and nature has been called a religion by many analysts.[13] We could also point to the fairly widespread reformation attempts within the Christian churches since the Renaissance, and similar reformations in other areas of the world as the new knowledge of the different cultures and of modern science has disturbed the equilibrium of their religions with their traditional patterns of life.

Inside or outside the traditional religions, the Marxist reformation has certainly been the most impressive in terms of the rapid extension of its mission around the world. But, as Kluckhohn has already pointed out, it is not a very adequate religion.[14] The Marxist program of salvation is weakened by the failure of the Marxist myth and cult to incorporate the still valid and necessary wisdom of the long-tested traditional religions and its failure to incorporate much new information from the sciences in the past century that is highly relevant for human values. So, even though the demand for a credible faith for personal and social salvation is tremendous, I do not believe that the Marxist myth is adequate for the production of human attitudes and behavior that will be selected by the powers or realities that select or judge human history.

I should insert here a note about my seriousness in using the term "myth" to denote both traditional religious myths and contemporary scientific theories. The term "myth" has a pejorative connotation for many today, as meaning something that is not really true. But many modern scientists hold their scientific hypotheses and theories likewise to be imaginative stories. I had the good fortune to sit for some years at the feet of the late physicist and philosopher of science, Philipp Frank. He helped make clear that "science is not a picture of the real world but a symbolic system [myth] by which our experiences can be correlated to each other in a practical way."[15]

I use the term "myth" in this sense to refer to the imaginative hypotheses of the sciences as well as to those of primitive or contemporary theology. The primary difference in the quality or validity of the myths lies in the way in which the scientific myths are systematically tested out in the world of common experience, a kind of forced "natural selection." There is also a difference in the purpose of the scientific and religious myths, in that a myth to be religious is always required to answer some religious concern —to say something significant about man's ultimate concerns, his purposes and meaning and the requirements laid upon him by reality if he is to find life and that more abundantly as a member of the human community. The scientific myth is constrained only to provide a picture of some aspect of experience or "reality," not necessarily to provide a picture of its value or meaning for human life. That is the function of religion. But I see no reason why both systems of myths, all systems of myths, should not be integrated. In fact, it would seem that in past human cultures this has been the case. In fact, it has been held to be a necessary characteristic of a coherent and effective culture that it have a unifying and credible myth or world view. In 1956, John Ely Burchard, then president of the American Academy of Arts and Sciences, said: "It seems to me a most challenging obligation of an academy of all the arts and sciences in the middle of this explosive century to explore more effective means of communication among the many different fields of learning, particularly communications that can yield proper perspective for a general world view. Somehow one cannot help but presume that all great civilization depends on some kind of basically coherent view that provides a common basis for the rational and successful handling of the problems it faces, whether or not such a view is explicit or only implicit among the people."[16] It is my prophecy that we will not be able to sustain our present scientific-technological interdependent world culture for long unless such a myth, world view, or body of common sacred belief begins to grasp the minds and feelings of significant fractions of the populations of the world.

The religious art or techne is vital to our survival and our further evolution as humans. The emptiness, the impotence, and the "God is dead" character of many of our higher religions has already been sensed by many in the younger generation as yielding only an intolerable meaningless and a void or confusion of fundamental values. They often are turning to primitive or foreign religious cults in their search for a myth of meaning and value that they have come to sense as necessary. While they may find some temporary comfort in a regression to earlier cults and sampling of alien forms of religious culture, many of them do not yet know that this will not be sufficient for coping with a highly modern, scientific, technological, world culture. For such a culture to survive, religious technology must keep pace with scientific technology, and theology must keep pace with the sciences over which she is rightfully (and ultimately, necessarily) queen, by virtue of her being defined as the science dealing with man's supreme or ultimate concerns. If a sufficient portion of the youth, alienated from effective religious and cultural values, are not for very long enchanted by esoteric or primitive myths, nor are by drugs made more sensitive and given more rational powers to cope, it is possible that those who have not yet destroyed themselves may in rage and panic turn to destroy both the good and bad of the culture. This sort of thing is already occurring with increasing frequency.

If we were to take the perspective of some superanthropologists from Mars in the year 2000 seeking to analyze what made earthmen of the twentieth century tick, we might hear them say, talking in general-systems language, that human societies were systems with memories dually transmitted by their genotypes and by their culture types, which served to define and maintain the organization of humanity as a group of subsystems in an ecosystem of planet Earth. For men, everything seemed to be progressing quite well for more than a million years up until the end of the second millennium A.D. But then a rapid explosion of the sciences began to inform everything human societies did, to inform all the arts of men, except for those arts which shaped men's basic attitudes toward themselves, their societies, and their ecosystem—their religious and moral values. The technology of value-attitude formation had become so obsolete and neglected by the end of the twentieth century that people began to believe there was no objective, universal, religious, and moral truth. Everything seemed relative. Individuals felt that only their own personal desires were the standards for value: existential, situational, hedonistic, and individual values. They had forgotten or never were taught about a nonhuman or superhuman reality that has established the values to which all men must conform. Earlier beliefs in transcendent gods or powers were dead. Hence the more advanced societies, where faith in the gods died first, began to decay within; their youth felt that life had no meaning, and they increasingly became disoriented and alienated with respect to the reality of the society that spawned them, and their random, senseless, hedonist behavior destroyed the society's organization and self-control. There were some less advanced societies, where a sociocultural idealism still flourished. But the more primitive societies had inherited from the more advanced societies the doomsday explosive power of the technology of atomic energy, which, along with their own overweening nationalism, led them in their conflicts with one another to push the button that brought on the atomic holocaust that brought an end to Homo sapiens.

Any number of scenarios of the next decades could be written, all ending in a tragedy because the people had lost their vision and their awareness of the reality that transcends their own private desires, a reality from the judgment of which they cannot escape; or because their vision of the ultimate judge was not one pertinent to the new realities, such as atomic power that they held in their hands. In any case, while many such tragic outcomes to human history as a result of technological revolutions are possible by the year 2000, my preachment to a theological school contemplating the trends of technology and values in the twenty-first century is that the trend and outcome of all technologies depend upon one central technology, the technology that provides the input of ultimate values or fundamental attitudes into a society.

Notes

1. One of the best statements I know on living systems is that of three papers by James G. Miller, formerly director of the Mental Health Research Institute of the University of Michigan, and currently vice-president of Cleveland State University. These papers entitled "Living Systems" were published in *Behavioral Science,* Vol. 10 (1965), pp. 193–237 and 337–411. The author has informed me that they are to be included with related material in a book.

2. E.g., Alfred E. Emerson, "Dynamic Homeostasis: A Unifying Principle in Organic, Social, and Ethical Evolution," *Zygon, Journal of Religion and Science,* Vol. III, No. 2 (June, 1968), pp. 129–168.

3. For instance, see this fact well developed in such places as Theodosius Dobzhansky's *Mankind Evolving* (Yale University Press, 1962) and Emerson in the previous note.

4. Donald T. Campbell, in an unpublished manuscript distributed to a graduate course at Northwestern University, winter, 1970.

5. For instance, see Walter B. Canon, *The Wisdom of the Body* (W. W. Norton & Company, Inc., 1932).

6. Anthony F. C. Wallace, "Religious Revitalization: A Function of Religion in Human History and Evolution," paper presented at the 8th Conference on Religion in an Age of Science at Star Island, off Portsmouth, New Hampshire, July 26, 1961. Also in Anthony F. C. Wallace, *Religion: An Anthropological View* (Random House, Inc., 1966), p. 38–39.

7. R. B. Lindsay, *The Role of Science in Civilization* (Harper & Row, Publishers, Inc., 1963).

160

8. E.g., Harlow Shapley, *Of Stars and Men* (Beacon Press, Inc., 1958).

9. Erwin Schrödinger, *What Is Life? and Other Scientific Essays* (Doubleday and Company, Inc., 1956).

10. Norbert Wiener, *Human Use of Human Beings: Cybernetics and Society* (Houghton Mifflin Company, 1950).

11. Lindsay, *op. cit.,* pp. 291–292.

12. See, for example, Miller, *loc. cit.,* and Kenneth E. Boulding, *The Meaning of the Twentieth Century* (Harper Colophon Books, 1964). J. Bronowski's "New Concepts in the Evolution of Complexity: Stratified Stability and Unbounded Plans" is published in *Zygon,* Vol. V, No. 1 (March, 1970), pp. 18–35, and is followed by a commentary by me on pp. 36–40. My quotations here come largely from pp. 32–33. Aharon Katchalsky, who is Director of the Polymer Research Laboratory of the Weizmann Institute of Science in Rehovoth, Israel, will publish a paper on "Thermodynamics of Flow and Biological Organization" in an as yet undesignated issue of *Zygon* in 1971. The quotation I make here is from a letter to me dated September 13, 1968. There is a large body of scientific literature that provides bridges among the phenomena and conceptual elements permeating physics, biology, sociology, and psychology. The citations I make are simply "for examples" that come to mind from some of those I happen to know best.

13. For instance, see Clyde Kluckhohn, "The Scientific Study of Values and Contemporary Civilization," *Zygon,* Vol. I, No. 3 (September, 1966), pp. 230–243.

14. *Ibid.,* especially pp. 232–233.

15. See the memorandum signed by Philipp Frank in *Daedalus,* Vol. 87, No. 4 (Spring, 1958), pp. 158–160. A number of us in the American Academy of Arts and Sciences subsequently sought to bring off a conference on the kinship of scientific and religious myths, but the position of the scientists was not understood and the hoped-for rapprochement of the sciences with the arts and humanistic scholarship was not made. This latter is partly reflected in the introduction by Henry Alexander Murray to the issue of *Daedalus* (and the later book) where the conference papers were published. See *Daedalus,* Vol. 88, No. 2 (Spring, 1959), p. 218.

16. This was quoted in "Notes from the Academy" in *Daedalus,* Vol. 87, No. 4 (Fall, 1958), p. 155.

CHAPTER VIII

Prophecies
of a Scientific Theology

Ralph Wendell Burhoe

Every art or technology is the application of some skill, information, knowledge, understanding, or science to some human need, goal, or value, real or imagined. Many people confuse science and technology. Landing a man on the moon is not science, but technology. To be sure, there would be no technology to land a man on the moon were there not a science, including the equations for the motions of the planets. Chemistry is not medicine, but it may be applied in the medical use of chemicals to satisfy a human value, such as to stop a pain or remove a dangerous growth. From this it should be clear that science or knowledge alone does not create technology, and science does not make any technology until men understand that the science is relevant to fulfilling their needs or values and then apply the science to this end. Thus, we cannot predict the future of technology until we can predict men's felt needs or values. Man does not *apply* knowledge (develop a technology) until he feels a need to which the application of the knowledge provides a solution.

But men's felt values, as we have noted in the previous chapter, are in considerable degree shaped by their religious beliefs. Beliefs about what is of ultimate or basic concern are by their very nature the keys to the hierarchy of human values. Insofar as religions have indeed been effective in transmitting in a population its basic beliefs and ultimate concerns, the religions have determined the values and hence the technologies.

For instance, it is quite clear that the knowledge or science that informs contraceptive technology will result in different technologies in different religious societies. Among the Protestants and agnostics contraceptive technologies of certain kinds have flourished. Among the Roman Catholics, the Shakers, and certain other religious groups around the world, contraceptive technology has been very different, even when their cultures had access to the same scientific information. Current moral and religious values will determine what technologies people will build with atomic energy (bombs or cancer cures or both), what they will do with knowledge of how to travel in space, with knowledge of how to wash brains, and in every other realm of potential technology, except a more effective religion. The values of a Thoreau could lead him to reject much contemporary technology. The scientist who informs men how to make television does not determine the programs that are broadcast. The programs are determined by the dominant values held by the paying public or by whatever other controlling agents that are allowed by the value-setting political-economic system of the public.

Since the trend and the future state of the religious art or technology in the year 2000 will have more to say about the state of human values than all other technologies (because the supreme values in the value hierarchy determine the direction of the others), let us now turn to consider in more detail the nature of the future religious art or technology which includes the theology or science that informs it.

If Religion Is a Technology, Is There a Science to Inform it?

It should be kept in mind that here I am using the term "religious art or technology" to refer to the total human enterprise that we call religious, to the total human enterprise that does apply information or skill in the producing of such desired ends as the salvation of individuals, or societies of individuals, with respect to their ultimate concerns, needs, or values. Also, I am confining my attention to religion as an art or technology of a cultural tradition. I am not considering the genetic and other physiological roots of unique, individual, religious experiences that are not in any way influenced by a cultural tradition. There are in fact no cases of individual religious experience apart from their being structured or patterned by a cultural heritage any more than there is in man a private language apart from its being structured or patterned by a cultural heritage. A feral child cannot speak a language, for the input of a cultural tradition is the only way he could inherit one. No individual in a single lifetime has the capacity to build a language from scratch; language-building for computers or Esperanto depends on a tremendous inheritance from other languages. Religions, like languages, depend on a complex cultural heritage, and there are no religions that are not built on such a heritage. I emphasize this "cultural art or technology" characteristic of religion because it is from the point of view of a scientific study of religion a good way of expressing a fundamental characteristic of the nature of religion and also it is, from the point of view of understanding how a religion might become scientifically informed, a good way of showing the parallel between science and any of the arts or technologies where science has been applied.

As Wallace said, religion "attempts to elucidate and describe the organization of self and cosmos," and this for the purpose of "maximizing the quantity of organization in the matrix of human experience." Let me provide some exegesis of this important statement by saying that religion communicates to its adherents a description of vital elements of the reality of the self and of the world that are ordinarily hidden to normal vision. Religious myths are like the sciences, and are indeed the earliest forms of science, in that they provide imaginative hypotheses about nonobvious or even invisible entities to explain the state of self and the world as we find them. That also might be as good a definition of science as you will get: an imaginative hypothesis or model of nonobvious or invisible entities to explain the states of the world (including self) as we find it. Hypotheses about electrons, atoms, genes, retinal molecules, and electroencephalograms are about nonobvious or invisible entities which go a long way to explain many things about the states of the world and man as we find them.

We must note that some anthropologists, although not all, argue that in each religious culture at the time of its beginning or of its reformations there is harmony or congruence between religious beliefs and the general or secular state of beliefs of the society the religion serves.[1] That is, there is no separation of the secular and sacred at the epistemic level. The credibility and validation of the gods of the thunderstorm were about as great to the populations where they first arose (or still flourish) as the credibility and validation of most scientific hypotheses, such as those about the atoms, the Wegener hypothesis of continental drift, or the phlogiston and caloric hypotheses where they have been believed.

To the extent these theories about the history of ideas, religious and secular, are true, to that extent it is clear that theology is a science relative to which religion is the art or technology; and that the science of religion (theology) is related to the practice of religion in the same way that the science of medicine is related to the practice of medicine, or the various engineering sciences are to the various arts or technological practices of engineering.

It is well documented that it was not until the last century that the pure sciences had much of any impact on technologies.[2] Theology and astronomy were notable exceptions, where the arts of religion and navigation were in many cases highly dependent upon their sciences. But most of our technology at the beginning of this century did not owe too much to scientific theory. Sailing with sails was a technology long before man understood the aerodynamics that explains it, and similarly with agriculture, metallurgy, steam engines, and countless other technologies. The use of fire has been an effective and significant technology for hundreds of thousands of years; and it was only a couple of centuries ago when we began to understand some of its grosser physical ingredients and only in the past century some of its finer physical characteristics. The history of technology and science show there is a long interdependence of the two areas, with practice or application or technology coming usually prior to theory or pure science.

This is an interesting parallel to the history and some of the debate going on in anthropology as to which came first in human cultures: myths or rituals. Both this and the question of whether science preceded technology are akin to the question of which came first, the hen or the egg. For the evolutionary theorists these kinds of questions are no problem, for they are all part of a perpetual negative feedback circuit where a memory selected from past experience is fed back into the circuit (together with a small amount of mutation or random variation) that leads to a new soma or body or experiment which is again tested or judged or selected by the ecological niche where the system is operating, thus the feedback input is either rejected or maintained. By such a circuit we can describe the trials and errors of a baby learning to walk or to see, the trials and errors of the evolution of the hen and the egg, the trials and errors of the evolution of a science and its technical applications, and the trials and errors of a religious myth or theology and the corresponding religious practices.

But the point of great significance is that in just the past century there has been an explosion in the realm of knowing that has ushered in a new age, the like of which has never before occurred on earth. The grand scientific formulations such as those of electromagnetic, thermodynamic, quantum mechanics, etc., have led to highly realistic logical or symbolic models of some hidden realities of the world. These models work so well that the rate of technological invention is no longer dependent on very slow trials and errors, but leap profusely, often full-born out of the heads, so to speak, of scientists, or scientifically trained men. The last century of the second millennium A.D. is the dawn of a radically new age. Man has literally risen above the earth to ascend into the heavens because of the revelations of the sciences. But spiritually he is in sore straits.

While in the past century the medical, agricultural, manufacturing, communications, military, and other arts or technologies have been fantastically enriched by the tremendous new power of the scientific myths or hypotheses, the religious arts around the world have been declining in power and relevance because of their seeming irrelevance in a scientifically informed world. I shall not go into the partially good reasons for the turn of Christian theology, following World War I, away from liberalism and away from the sciences. The neo-orthodox movement, while it could be praised for its proper critique of some shortcomings of the old liberalism, was itself running into a blind alley in asserting the irrelevance of science for theology.

Because of smiliar tendencies in different ways today, there is still some question in my mind whether the traditional theological community or the new existential zealots will take advantage of the new scientific revelations for their rich potentialities for application to the queen of human concerns, namely, the ulimate or religious concerns. It may be that some nonchurch agencies will move ahead faster, such as community mental health, social welfare centers, the socialist parties, or groups like those described by Mowrer. They already are increasingly preempting the church's functions, and conceivably could become the "religious" institutions of the future. However, it is still my bet that at several points in the next few years and decades the traditional theological and religious communities will find the scientific revelations a gold mine, and that by early in the third millennium A.D. a fantastic revitalization and universalization of religion will sweep the world. The ecumenical power will come from a universalized and credible theology and related religious practices, not from the politics of dying institutions seeking strength in pooling their weaknesses.

Let us look at some of the potentials for a theology informed positively by the sciences. While some of the present theologians are selling their birthright—their claims to interpret the gifts and demands of the almighty transcendent Lord of creation—there is beginning to arise in the twentieth century a group of scientists who are seers of the unseen hand that rules human destiny. These men have not been very much heard, seen, or understood by the general public or by the religious communities. I have quoted a bit from some of them. The public, and to some extent the churches, have heard at least a bit of what the ecologists have to say; and there is a growing concern that it is a moral duty to quit overpolluting and overpopulating the earth. Gradually, the grow-

ing wisdom of the scientific seers or prophets will probably ⌐
through to leaders of the Christian community as significant confirmations and extensions of their historic faith. For in reality
these scientists are declarers of what the transcendent reality will
permit and what it will reject, and hence what is good or bad for
each and every living being or system, and what man must do to
be saved for fulfillment in higher levels of order or organization
or life. I prophesy that from this source man is most likely to find
an enlarged vision of purpose and hope, for the credible myth of
human meaning in the scheme of things.

What I am trying to suggest here is that the art of religion, like
the technology or art of medicine, will be best informed and most
able to function adequately in an age of radically new science and
technology when that religion is itself informed by currently credible knowledge provided by the sciences. You may soon be hearing of the resident cosmologist, the resident evolutionist, the resident behaviorist at theological schools, as well as the resident psychologists, psychiatrists, and sociologists. But, as I have pointed
out in another place, while some of the psychotherapeutic technology has been welcomed at theological schools, there has been
little genuine integration of systematic theology with the scientific
world views even of the main schools of the psychiatric profession.[3] There is not much talk about God with the psychiatrists.
This is in contrast with what is going on in medicine, where
mathematicians, physicists, chemists, biologists, psychologists, and
scientists of all kinds are involved in the development of the new
"doctrines" (theories) and "rituals" (practices) that are making
the medical arts modern, credible, and salvatory in the twentieth
century.

The analogy of scientific religion with scientific medicine must
not be misunderstood as suggesting that religion would be mixed
in a test tube and taken as a pill, perhaps to produce a "religious
experience." Some have in fact recommended taking LSD for this
purpose. But such a "religious experience" is only a small corner
of the totality of the complex system that is religion, even if—as
rarely happens—it should turn out to be a useful, valid, or viable
religious experience. For a scientific religion, we need to consider

a full picture of the nature and function of religion that is informed by the various resources of religious scholarship, including theologians, historians, anthropologists, sociologists, psychologists, and others. I am therefore thinking of religion as including (1) a system of beliefs about the ultimate nature and meaning of man and his relation to whatever are the ultimate realities on which his life and destiny depend; and (2) the institutions that store and transmit (or teach) the belief system and utilize it in a schedule of observances, rites, dramas, readings, sermons, and other means of helping individuals to structure their attitudes and behaviors in ways beneficial for their own private as well as for the general welfare and satisfaction. The beliefs and observances (or practices) operate to establish the characteristic values or goals of the religion as norms within each individual. A scientifically informed religion would seek to utilize the "truths" of the sciences in reforming its system of beliefs to make it more credible and effective for the religion's own purposes: to provide man with salvatory orientations, attitudes, goals, or values with respect to the ultimately significant aspects of himself, his fellowmen, and the total reality in which he lives.

How different would be the authority and credibility of the religious profession and the salvatory power of its ministries, did they share in the credible myths the medical profession has found in all the sciences. As James Gustafson[4] pointed out, while the medicos can rejoice at every new discovery in the sciences, the plight of the clergyman is fear that even more of his authority and credibility will disappear. But, for some understandable but now unfortunate historical causes, the bulk of religious professionals from the time of Galileo to that of Darwin and Freud and today have raised their hackles and excommunicated the ideas of scientists when they seemed to reveal a different world view from that in which the world or man was portrayed in the centuries when the Christian Scriptures were written. There was some justification for this, and there still is. But there are many disadvantages, the major one being the dissolution of the faith or belief in the whole message of religion because of its expression in an outmoded picture of the world and man.

The list of constructive integrators of science with theology is growing. A most creative spirit was the Jesuit paleontologist, Père Pierre Teilhard de Chardin, who, in my opinion, probably did more for a truly ecumenical faith and theology single-handedly than all the ecumenically oriented political councils of his church combined. This impact may not be verified for a few decades yet, but I think such might be the judgment of historians in the next century. Teilhard moved in the direction of integrating the evolutionary doctrine of man with his church's theology; he went a long way in this direction. While, as some social scientists and historians have pointed out, the ecumenical overtures on organizational or institutional levels are often furtive reachings for reinforcements in the midst of retreat, and not really a sign of growth or power, Teilhard has appealed deeply across the board to Protestants and Catholics and to secular scientists such as Sir Julian Huxley or Theodosius Dobzhansky. He has not provided an adequate integration either from the scientific or from the theological side, but he has blazed a trail. He has many critics from both camps, although I think the critics often have failed to understand him. It is still a difficult area in which to make sense because of traditional prejudices.

Scientists Turning Theologians

But what is perhaps of greater importance to those who would develop a credible, enlightening, and effectively motivating belief for the confused, unstable, and sometimes mad individuals and mobs developing within the small confines of Spaceship Earth is the basis for theology that is growing within the scientific community, often among men who have no serious affiliation within a traditional church or religion. I have already mentioned some of the fruits of such scientists for providing us grounds and rationale for a doctrine of church, for the essentiality of religion, and for its essential superiority (sometimes even in its traditional form) over a lot of the recent psychosociological prescriptions on basic human values. I have just shown how such scientists are showing that religion is universal, and that in abstract form or generic definition it is as invariant and necessary in human culture as central nervous systems are in higher animals. It will be with us in the twenty-first century if we are here. Without an adequate religion for the whole new worldwide culture of Spaceship Earth, we may not be here in the twenty-first century, or perhaps historians from other parts of the cosmos would find only some dying remnants of human or other life on earth.

But I have gone farther to suggest that some positive notions about invariants that are transcendent to man and that inhere in the reality in which we live are being revealed by the sciences, such as the basic command to all life, including the highest levels of human life, of the *thermodynamic imperative*. We may say that scientists have begun to reveal or unveil some objective "thou shalts" and "thou shalt nots." Let me give a couple more examples of serious theological concern by some outstanding scientists.

Biologist Garrett Hardin wrote:

> In the minds of most laymen, and indeed of many scientists, science is primarily an activity in which one discovers how to do today what was yesterday thought impossible; for many, science is a faith that nothing is impossible. But to the more profound students of the philosophy of science such a faith is impiety. The history of science may quite properly be . . . correctly interpreted as the search for the definition of the impossibilities of this world. Edmund Whittaker, a mathematical physicist, has called these the *impotence principles*. . . .
>
> We are terribly clever people, we moderns: we bend Nature to our will in countless ways. We move mountains . . . fly at speeds no other organism can achieve, and tap the power of the atom. We are terribly clever. The essentially religious feeling of subserviency to a power greater than ourselves comes hard to us clever people. But by our intelligence we are now beginning to make out the limits to our cleverness, the impotence principles that say what can and cannot be. In an operational sense, we are experiencing a return to a religious orientation toward the world.[5]

We should note that the miracles that Professor Hardin referred to, such as moving mountains or flying into the heavens, are miracles that are by the popular mind ascribed to science, but which in more exact language is technology. But the main point that he

makes, and that many other scientists are making in many different ways, is that the scientific view of man is not one where man
is master of his destiny and can do whatever he likes. The reality
that created and sustains us forbids many things, some of which
we sometimes make the mistake of thinking we like or need or
value. There is a widespread heresy or misunderstanding of science and technology that is from the point of view of good scientists truly nonsensical: namely, that, from here on, science puts
man in control of his own evolution, so that he can make his own
destiny. A lot of people have come to believe this, including
churchmen whose predecessors used to think that human destiny
was in the hands of the Lord, and including scientists whose science pictures man's fate as determined by natural causes. Even
such a careful writer and knowledgeable scientist as Sir Julian
Huxley has committed this kind of error. The real fact is, as Sir
Julian knows better than most, that man never did create himself
or determine his own values, but man ultimately owes all he is
to events beyond his own nature. His present nature is the product of more than a billion-year long and complex history guided
by an external, nonhuman ("transcendent") reality that has
shaped his destiny.

As Professor Gilkey pointed out in Chapter IV by quoting
anthropologist Julian Steward, the faith that human destiny is
determined by forces external and superior to man is as much a
faith of the social and behavioral scientists as it is of the physical
and biological: "science must proceed *as if* natural laws operate
consistently and without exception, as if all cultures and all aspects
of human behavior had determinants." In any lengthy chain of
analysis, these forces or determinants lie outside of the individual
man or the particular society or culture that is being "explained."
Ultimately they are all nonhuman forces. Since they do determine
human destiny, they are in fact superior or transcendent to man in
power. Because ultimately we cannot trace them to infinity and
we are forced to remain ignorant of ultimates, these forces that
determine human destiny are transcendent in that they lie beyond
the limits of human experience or knowledge. There is a striking
resemblance between theological determinism or predestination

and the scientific faith in the hypothesis of determinism, between the rule of an "almighty God" and the lawful evolution of cosmic processes.

While it is true that many scientists, in their efforts to interpret science for the public and for their own private living, have pointed to man's new levels of understanding and his consequent new powers for enriching life, and while some of them occasionally become overenthusiastic or careless and imply that ultimate power or value lies in man, it has been my experience in a lifetime of living among scientists that few among them would say that man can lift himself by his own bootstraps, that man created himself, that man can determine his own destiny. The error that makes it appear that science says that man dominates nature and is free to determine his own destiny comes from applying a statement of one level of analysis to another level where it does not apply.

There is no doubt that, at the level of certain finite problems, the new knowledge from the sciences about how things work or might work under natural laws has enabled new and better technological solutions for many human needs in food, medicine, living facilities, transport, communications, and in most every area of life. Hence the new knowledge does give man new powers to control natural events and processes in ways that fulfill human needs. Logically it would seem that one could keep adding such small steps toward the fulfillment of human desires, and hence conclude that man is master of his fate and can control nature to fulfill all his desires. But this logic overlooks a basic presupposition of the sciences: that the natural laws are universal and apply also to what makes men desire and behave the way they do. Here, instead of man being master of nature, he must recognize his master.

I would guess that most good scientists, especially those who know about what makes man tick, would concur with the sentiment of ancient Biblical theology that says "unless the Lord builds the house [that is, in more scientific language, unless the builders operate in accord with what the nature of things will permit], the builders do labor in vain." I think they would agree with another bit of Biblical theology: that man holds whatever minor and finite powers he has over nature only by virtue of the fact that his Creator thus endowed man with such power. Each living creature's powers (including man's) come thanks to the cumulated information stored in his genotype, culture, and nervous system that gives him the know-how for doing such things as will enable him to extract his needs from the gifts for maintaining life that are available in the environing nature.

A man's power over his own nature and over environing nature is, if you will, the cosmic nature's (the "Lord's") wisdom incarnated in man. It should be noted that man never violates (overcomes or nullifies) scientific, natural law. That is impossible. He may try to do something that he believes will violate natural law, such as to jump off a cliff in the hope that he will be able to fly. But the law of gravity operates regardless. Man cannot violate that law, even when he flies over the moon. He flies over the moon only when he knows enough about the natural laws and the actual boundary conditions of the situation so that he can adapt or conform to them well enough to accomplish his purpose. Thus, man can never conquer nature. On the contrary, man's own fulfillment of his desires, needs, or values for existence as a living system or being comes only in the measure that he finds and incarnates in himself the boundary conditions and laws of nature that spell out what is required.

Thus, if a scientist writes about some capacities or powers that knowledge gives man, he is really writing about what man can do when he does properly incarnate or represent the laws and elements of the cosmos that yield the homeostatic conditions of life—not because he can violate or triumph over them. He may triumph over the barren desert to grow a crop, but only because he is obedient to the larger law of irrigating it, for the law of plant life requires water. There is no triumph over this law, no possibility of successfully defying the laws of the objective reality. It is true that some scientists sometimes fail to mention this fact—especially when they are speaking of the minor miracles such as watering the desert, healing diseases, or flying over the moon—that it is only obedience to nature's laws that makes it possible. There is no doubt, as Schilling points out, that "a splendid future will surely come if man labors *with* God." There are many scientists who would say that the cosmos or nature that they perceive is tantamount to what religious people have been calling God.

However, there are many elaboraters of the myths of scientific utopia who do not seem to understand man's finitude and impotence before the sovereign Lord of nature. There are millions today who preach and millions who believe that technological man can manipulate his environment to please himself, and that he himself is his own master and his own savior. This is contrary to the basic scientific doctrine of determinism, to the scientific faith that events, including events in human life, can be explained in terms of natural sequences in history according to some universal laws of nature.

The scientific pictures tell me that all our powers and capacities for life have come to us by the grace of cosmic and earthly processes in history, a grace that we can properly call transcendent, and awe-inspiring for man's finite mind to contemplate. I think that most good scientists I have known agree that about ultimates in cosmic history, or even the ultimates of the present moment, we know nothing. Even the principles of invariance that I have been talking about are, more strictly termed, principles that have far-reaching invariance. In our own recent intellectual history, we have had to keep revising even such relatively great invariances as Newton's laws. It is as if the enterprise of science, like the enterprise of the evolution of life, is one of imposing a small degree of invariance or order on the surrounding chaos; but we soon find that the comprehensiveness of our pattern of order is terribly finite in an infinite ocean of chaos, so that we are constantly revising and reforming as our patterns of order evolve increasingly to correspond, adapt, or fit the realities of the infinity around us. Perhaps we can say our ultimate goal value is to seek and to incarnate that which is indeed ultimate and invariant in the flux of time.

Not only was our creation a gift of grace, but our new powers to do things in the world, our fantastic new technological powers, are not really different. These new powers only come to us when we incorporate in our own nature and behavior the rules and conditions inherent in the transcendent reality which created us and sustains us. Of all the things that we might wish to do, we can only do a very small fraction. Even then we can only do them if our wishes conform to an external reality that transcends us.

Perhaps a lot of what I am suggesting as a possible avenue for a significant theological and religious revitalization to guide the people of the world in the new millennium is summarized in the words of the rather unchurchly and unorthodox astronomer, Harlow Shapley.

Cosmic evolution is my central theme. Anthropomorphism and anthropocentrism are false images of reality and man's place in it. If we could accept cosmic evolution, and could get away from the more primitive projections of our own images, religions and philosophies would be richer and truer. By anthropocentrism I mean the state of being personally blinded by a presumption of our own cosmic importance—a belief in the existence of a universe centered on terrestrial genus *Homo*. Once we are free from that man-centered illusion, our minds can roam over a universe that, in size, power, and meaning, puts our traditional vanities to modesty if not to shame.

We have evidence of a truly wide Cosmic Evolution from hydrogen to *Homo,* and probably somewhere an evolution beyond the *Homo* level of sentiency. We have in Cosmic Evolution a fundamental principle of growth that affects the chemical atoms as well as plants and animals, the stars and nebulae, space-time and mass-energy. In brief, everything that we can name, everything material and non-material, is involved. It is around this Cosmic Evolution that we might build revised philosophies and religions.

To advance further . . . , it is clear that our emphasis in a program for life should turn away more and more from the animal—turn, shall I say, toward the angelic. If you are allergic to angels, turn then toward the spiritual—spiritual, broadly spoken.

Where and why does religion come into the cosmic picture? Is it one of the rewards and penalties of human societal organizations? Or is it merely a product of the restless human mind? The anthropologists report that all tribes, including our own, have religions of some sort. Religion seems to evolve with questioning brains and new social requirements. Curiosity breeds explanatory hypotheses or beliefs. Human brains or minds require at least hypothetical answers to questions that concern them. Historical evidence suggests that religious beliefs came before scientific beliefs in providing hypotheses about the nature of the world and man's place in it. The beliefs about the customs or laws of the spirits and gods explained to earlier men what it is they are required to do to have the best of life.

But can we have better beliefs today? I have already suggested that the scientific pictures of Nature, the Nature which the sciences reveal, are the best or most reliable explanations that we have. I have suggested that even for the sciences there are many mysteries and unknowns at the frontiers of our hypothetical explorations and explanations. We do not yet know very much about our own nature and nearly nothing about the ultimates of existence; but we do and seemingly ever can know more about the inclusive Nature that produced us and presumably produces even higher patterns of life elsewhere in the evolving cosmos. For us higher primates at the forefront of living systems on earth, perhaps the best guide for the life we hold dear may come from a closer search for the potentialities which this inclusive Nature may hold for us.

Although it may not seem to you to be a full definition of God, it is to many quite satisfying to equate Nature and God. My phrase, now too well known, that "All Nature is God and all God is Nature," is a pantheistic statement that is, I believe, completely operable. A shorter version is "Nature is God and God is Nature." Still shorter, and deeply meaningful, is: "Nature is All." That last presents the essence of Natural Piety.[6]

I suggest that natural piety coming out of such impious men is a growing trend. I think our new theologies and our new pietistic poetry will become enriched from such sources. This enrichment is not the nostalgic piety found in some scientists of the past hundred years who wrote a word in favor of religion as they grew old. I am calling attention to a vigorous and very gripping public concern and piety that come straight out of insights from their science, and provide a credibility that could revitalize religious piety. I could list dozens of books and articles of this type written in the last couple of decades.[7]

The most scientific and credible cosmic myths about man and his destiny in my opinion tend to fit in with what theologians call

"God talk." While some theologians may not like the character of the God thus revealed, it is a very credible picture of the source of man's being and the determiner of his destiny. Because of its credibility, because of the empirical evidence that such a God is indeed at work, it is my prophecy that it will prevail even though distasteful to the preferences of many people. As a matter of fact, the harshness of the Biblical God of the Old Testament was a characteristic that sent fear and trembling into the believers. The characteristics of the "ultimate reality" in religions generally is not dependent on whether men happen to like them. Gods are gods because of their superior power, not because men like what they do. The sovereign power of the "reality" symbolized by the sciences is godlike in this respect.

In the Epilogue, I shall say something about how religious symbols, reformed and translated into the language of the contemporary sciences may transform, reform, and revitalize world religions in a surprising new integration of a world-embracing common conviction or faith about personal and community values ordained by a reality that is sovereign overall in the cosmos; and about how such a faith may make possible the stability of the human species in a scientific and technological spaceship containing a few billion individuals.

Notes

1. See, for instance, Melford E. Spiro, "Religion and the Irrational," in *Proceedings* of the 1964 Annual Spring Meeting of the American Ethnological Society (University of Washington Press, 1964).

2. See, for instance, R. B. Lindsay, *The Role of Science in Civilization* (Harper & Row, Publishers, Inc., 1963), Chapter VII, "Science and Technology."

3. Burhoe, "Bridging the Gap Between Psychiatry and Theology," *Journal of Religion and Health,* Vol. VII, No. 3 (July, 1968), pp. 215–226; reprinted in *The Hourglass,* Vol. 2, Nos. 1–2 (1970).

4. Gustafson, "The Clergy in the United States," *Daedalus,* Vol. 92, No. 4 (Fall, 1963), pp. 724–744.

5. Garrett Hardin, *Nature and Man's Fate* (Holt, Rinehart & Winston, Inc., 1959), pp. 306 and 329.

6. Harlow Shapley, "Life, Hope, and Cosmic Evolution," *Zygon,* Vol. I, No. 3 (September, 1966), pp. 278–279, 281, 284–285, 279.

7. Here is a list of a couple of dozen books that represent the kind of writings about human values at the religious level which derive their power and inspiration largely from the authors' background in the sciences.

Barbour, Ian, *Science and Secularity: The Ethics of Technology.* Harper & Row, Publishers, Inc., 1970.

Barbour, Ian, *Issues in Science and Religion.* Prentice-Hall, Inc., 1966.

Bertalanffy, Ludwig von, *Robots, Men and Minds: Psychology in the Modern World.* George Braziller, Inc., 1968.

Birch, L. Charles, *Nature and God.* The Westminster Press, 1965.

Boulding, Kenneth E., *The Meaning of the 20th Century.* Harper & Row, Publishers, Inc., 1964.

Bronowski, Jacob, *Science and Human Values.* Julian Messner, Inc., 1956.

Commoner, Barry, *Science and Survival.* The Viking Press, Inc., 1966.

Coulson, C. A., *Science and the Idea of God.* London: Cambridge University Press, 1958.

Dobzhansky, Theodosius, *The Biology of Ultimate Concern.* The New American Library, 1967.

Dubos, René, *So Human an Animal.* Charles Scribner's Sons, 1968.

Eiseley, Loren C., *The Firmament of Time.* Atheneum, 1960.

Glass, Bentley, *Science and Ethical Values.* University of North Carolina Press, 1966.

Hardin, Garrett, *Nature and Man's Fate.* Holt, Rinehart & Winston, Inc., 1959.

Huxley, Julian S., *Religion Without Revelation.* Harper & Brothers, 1957.

Lindsay, R. B., *The Role of Science in Civilization.* Harper & Row, Publishers, Inc., 1963.

Margenau, Henry, *Ethics and Science.* D. Van Nostrand Company, Inc., 1964.

Mises, Richard von, *Positivism, A Study in Human Understanding,* tr. by Jerry Bernstein and Roger G. Newton. Harvard University Press, 1951.

Mowrer, O. H., *The Crisis in Psychiatry and Religion*. D. Van Nostrand Company, Inc., 1961.

Odom, Howard T., *Environment, Power, and Society*. Wiley—Interscience, 1971. Esp. Ch. 8 on "Energetic Basis for Religion."

Platt, John Rader, *The Step to Man*. John Wiley & Sons, Inc., 1966.

Polanyi, Michael, *Science, Faith and Society*. Oxford University Press, Inc., 1946.

Potter, Van R., *Bioethics: Bridge to the Future*. Prentice-Hall, Inc., 1971.

Rapoport, Anatol, *Science and the Goals of Man: A Study in Semantic Orientation*. Harper & Brothers, 1950.

Sabine, Paul E., *Atoms, Men and God*. Philosophical Library, Inc., 1953.

Schilling, Harold K., *Science and Religion*. Charles Scribner's Sons, 1962.

Shapley, Harlow, *Of Stars and Men*. Beacon Press, Inc., 1958.

Thorpe, W. H., *Science, Man and Morals*. Cornell University Press, 1967.

Waddington, C. H., *The Ethical Animal*. Atheneum, 1961.

Weizäcker, C. F. von, *The History of Nature*, tr. by Fred D. Wieck. London: Routledge & Kegan Paul, Ltd., 1951.

Twenty-first-Century Values from a Scientifically Based Theology That Creates a Common World Culture

Ralph Wendell Burhoe

This book on science and human values in the twenty-first century is at most a sketchbook. Its five authors from various areas of science and theology have responded from five different personal and professional perspectives. They have indicated that the institution of religion has a prominent role in the transmission of human values, historically at least. I have sided in some degree with the two who seem most certain of the centrality of religion still today, even of traditional Christian religion.

I have suggested that the term "religion" can be given a coherent and scientifically useful meaning when it is defined as the social institution that sets forth and transmits man's highest, most sacred, values, insofar as these require transmission through the culture type as well as genotype. This takes me beyond what many people would be willing to call religion. I join some of the psychosocial scientists and other scholarly analysts of human civilization to say that the Marxist-Communist or the psychotherapeutic ideologies are religious in character.

It was not long ago, and still is the case in some populations or societies that have not yet been opened to the budding, modern scientific-technological, world culture, that the infidel or nonreligious was anyone who did not believe in the same religious formulation that "our group" believes. But, with the growth of knowledge about other cultures, we have become accustomed to apply the term "religion" to all kinds of alien faiths. Some of us have come to see how various state faiths like Communism, Nazism, Socialism, Fascism, or Americanism are outgrowths or reformations of, or substitutes for, religious faiths, and are necessary as a minimal basis for the motivation of the population to community loyalty and cooperation. We are also generally ready to recognize, as was the case in the tale of the good Samaritan, that anyone who stops to help or heal another is a religious man, and this should include agnostic psychotherapists.

The question before us is, What will be the source and character of human values in the future? I prophesy that social institutions that are religious, that perform the same functions of transmitting the more sacred values of cultures, will continue in the twenty-first century to be the prime source of those values. I prophesy that very much of the ancient religious traditions will continue. I have suggested, on grounds akin to those I cited of psychologist Donald Campbell, that scientific or secular wisdom is not yet nearly advanced enough to provide fully adequate values for a viable culture. I prophesy, therefore, that the religious traditions which have been best tested or selected by the nature of circumstances in past history are going to be with us in the future insofar as future history provides similar circumstances. As Gilkey has pointed out, we are likely to have similar problems.

I have gone beyond this to point out that the sciences do not so much threaten as affirm religions when we view the nature and function of religions at more abstract and universal levels of language and understanding. For instance, I cited confirmation by scientists of that most central (although currently widely doubted) element of religious culture: God. Looking at the God concept in its basic, abstract, functional meaning—let us say, to name a few traditional characteristics of deity, God is the name of an objective reality far transcending man in time and space and power, which is the source (creator) of the world and men as we find them, a source apart from which man is nothing, a source that always has and always will determine human destiny—then it seems clear that many scientists and much of science has been revealing this reality. I have, therefore, sided with those theologians and others who think God talk is significant, and I do not see much sense in the "God is dead" theologians and others who would assert that human values are ultimately determined by man.

But I do not mean to suggest that the value-transmitting institutions of culture will remain unchanged. On the contrary, I have prophesied along with Jaspers and Wieman that we are in the beginning of the most radical religious reformation of all history. Religions evolve as do the other technologies of human cultures, and at critical times they evolve at a faster rate which we commonly call reformations.

Before coming to the nature of the present reformation, I want to make it clear that it is not the fundamental character of religion that will be changed, for I think we have properly analyzed (primarily in Chapter VII) the nature of religion on a level of abstraction that gives us the capacity to formulate its nature in a way that remains invariant regardless of the cultural variations in particular forms, just as we can speak of nourishment as an abstraction that remains invariant regardless of the cultural (or even organic) variations of this function.

In particular, I want to emphasize that in the current religious reformation the central and very ancient hypothesis or theory of religions will remain and be revitalized: the God concept, the concept that there is a power (or powers) superior to man, that created him and that will in the future as it has in the past determine his destiny, a dynamic reality operating in time that shapes us, that sets our values, that decrees what is good and evil, right and wrong, and from whose rulings we can never escape. In fact this concept is central both to theology and to science: the concept of causes outside or transcending ourselves which determine our destinies, causes which we are forced to accept and with which we have to learn to live on their terms. I will not here attempt to show that it is a fact that most of the religions of the world have focused their myths, symbols, or doctrines about such a notion of a transcendent ruling reality. I think I have made it clear (especially in Chapter VIII) that the sciences also proclaim such a transcendent reality.

Successions of Symbol Systems Don't Damage Deity but Do Confuse the Conceivers

I am now suggesting that religion remains religion and the nature of ultimate reality remains the nature of ultimate reality regardless of whether we speak in the symbols of primitive tribes, or of the Mediterranean world of 1000 B.C., or of A.D. 100 or 1000, or of the scientific-technological world of A.D. 2000. Whatever their stage of evolution, men always require information to structure their values, their notions of right and wrong, of good and evil. I have noted that the social institutions performing this function are commonly called religious, whether I use definitions of religion by theological apologists or by secular social scientists. That man's nature and his values are structured or set in the end by forces beyond himself has been recognized in most religions and in modern scientific pictures of man.

Now the connotation of any word or other symbol such as "god" or "man" changes as men's experience changes or evolves. We should note that modern science is very rapidly during the twentieth century providing new meanings for many words or symbols, and is giving the same or common meanings for these symbols to populations in what were once very diverse cultures with diverse world views. For the first time in history, men have had a mirror (or TV camera) held up to view the whole hemisphere of their world and have seen it reflected in their living rooms simultaneously all around the world. This is an augury for the spread to every man of a common but more detailed scientific view of himself and of his world. The scientific view of the "reality" is becoming the same in Paris and Peiping as in Pittsburgh. Barring the possibility of a disastrous disruption of the presently rapid spreading of the new universal world culture of science and technology, in the twenty-first century the new universal symbol system for comprehending the nature of man's own reality and of his world will have pretty well penetrated the perceiving and projecting mechanisms of the brains of the several billion men around the globe.

What is more important for us to note in making a prophecy is not that the science of 2000 or of 2100 will be the same as it is today, but that the science of either year will be basically the same for all men around the world. This does not mean that every man will perceive the complex detail of every science; but the sciences generally will provide a common world view that each individual will absorb up to the level of his capacities, interests, and needs. It will not be the world view of nineteenth-century Africans, of medieval Europeans, or of the Mediterranean basin, the Indian peninsula, or the expanses of China in the centuries of Socrates, the Hebrew prophets, Buddha, or Confucius.

Human values, human notions of good and evil and right and wrong, must be expressed in symbols or language that is credible and meaningful. Religious symbols, where they have been effective, have been in the common language or symbol system of the populations where they flourished. To be effective in the twenty-first century, human values must be expressed in the worldwide symbol system of the sciences. This means that in all religions of the world the doctrines of man and of the ultimate reality which determines his destiny will either be translated into the world view or symbol system of the sciences or else will become of diminishing credibility and effectiveness.

The twentieth century is one where this process of the breakup of local cultures of various levels or stages is in transition toward a universal, scientific culture. Many of the great religions are dying because their traditional symbol systems are dying among increasing fractions of the population as they are exposed to the new world views of the sciences. I prophesy that each of the religions will tend to be resurrected or revitalized and transformed as it effectively translates the viable wisdom of its tradition into this new symbol system of the sciences and as it reforms and extends the traditional wisdom to adapt human living to the requirements for living in the new one-world culture of increasingly closely interdependent billions of people on Spaceship Earth. This will provide a trend toward common visions of the ultimate realities on which man depends and of the ultimate goals of the one-world community. I have only briefly suggested in Chapter VIII how some notions of Western religion may be translated into the symbols of science. The details of the outcome of this process for either local or worldwide religions is not so important for us to recognize at first as is the fact that, so long as the scientific-technological world view continues to spread, natural selection as it operates in cultural evolution is going to weed out the religions that are unfit for motivating men to ordered or viable behavior in that world.

Weeding out of cultural patterns such as religions takes place first because of the religion's failure to communicate its message. If the population to which it speaks has no credence in its symbols —its gods and the rewards and punishments that they are alleged to mete out to men on the basis of men's obedience to or violation of the taboos or commands—then the population is not moved by the religion to follow its program for salvation.

The credence of a man in his religion is based on his most powerful desire, the desire for life, and this desire is heavily programmed by his genotype. This is the genetic base for religious devotion and for motivating morals. It is well known that men will believe almost anything that promises to satisfy their deepest longings, and religions customarily have done this. We can understand from this why sometimes flimsy and incredible myths are held so firmly.

But religious credence is also based on the evidence of experience. This evidence comes in several distinct forms. Psychology has shown that men find the apparent belief or approval of their fellowmen to be a very strong reason for believing or not believing something; if most of those I respect believe in hell, or that the world is round, so do I without bothering to investigate. Another form of evidence is whether a belief seems to be coherent with other beliefs one already holds, with what one remembers; religious beliefs about souls without bodies may violate neurophysiological theories and so be discounted. A third form of evidence is whether the outcomes that a belief promises do in fact come true and are actually experienced; if God is alleged to reward good behavior, and if Job or I do our best to behave well, and if in spite of this we are punished instead of rewarded, we may conclude that something is wrong with our notions of God or goodness or what we have done. Thus our wish to believe and our tendency to accept life-enriching religious promises is always being selected by various tests of credibility based on experience or empirical evidence. Religious beliefs are thus not basically separated from any other beliefs, except by their function to structure our values and hopes, and by the intensity of our need for them when we find our life or welfare threatened.

From the above, it should be clear that a system of religious beliefs that is integrated or coherent with the beliefs of contemporary science would be most likely to be credible. They would be believed by most of the community of people whose judgments and beliefs we respect; they would cohere with what we ourselves know of scientific beliefs; and they would most likely be found in experience to turn out as promised, since scientific beliefs and the predictions, or outcomes from scientific premises, have this reputation for being reliable.

For the same reasons, religious symbols (stories, myths, theologies, etc.) that fail to correspond in some good measure with the scientific world view will tend to be more and more discounted, and those religions will fail to communicate and hence will tend to have no effectiveness. When effectiveness is gone, the religion is dead. Thousands of historic religions are now dead, many more are dying.[1] Both historical and anthropological evidence indicate that religious "species" evolve and disappear, and, like biological species, only certain ones—those which adapt effectively to relating the reality or nature of man's religious needs to the larger reality on which he depends—survive. There is truth in the "God is dead" theology if you confine your concept of God to certain symbol systems that are no longer viable.

A religion may also fail even if it succeeds in communicating its message. Religions, like other technologies, may be better or worse in producing viability or life. It should never be forgotten that man's values are instruments of his viability. His attitudes toward himself, toward his fellowman, and toward his environment determine how well or poorly he as an individual, or his society as a cooperative unit on which each individual member is dependent, will adapt to the necessities for life and flourish. A religion that advocated total sexual abstinence would not survive even if it were effectively communicated and enacted. The more successfully it communicated its message the more certainly it would come to an end at the end of the generation now living. There are, of course, all sorts of intermediate degrees of validity of religions, once given the fact that they are credible and hence motivate people to believe and behave in accord with their particular program for salvation or life.

According to the theory propounded by psychologist Campbell,[2] the better religions would be selected over the less fit in any competition. The competition takes place whenever two different religious cultures come to communicate to the same population of men. History would seem to indicate that it is during these periods of new or increased impact of one culture on another that the great religious reformations come about, often raising one of the existing religions or some modification of it to a reigning position while the other competing religions tend to wither away.

Sometimes the impact of another culture is not direct from a living society or cult but from its nonliving seed, record, or memory in a rediscovered literature. This was the case in the religious reformations following the period of the Renaissance with its rediscovery of ancient literatures. The discovery and growth in America of some alien religion like Buddhism or Islam is sometimes more through the impact of a literature than through direct contact of imported living cults.

Regardless of how the competition takes place, the main point is that it does, even in isolated island societies. Among a dozen such isolated primitive societies, if half should happen by chance to adopt a religious or value pattern that will enable them to survive as a society for a few centuries in their ecological niches and if half fail to do this, one would expect that after the few centuries had passed a visitor from Mars or from some other culture, whose transport allowed him readily to go from one isolated island to the other, would find only the viable type of religions. The other islands would be uninhabited. Of course, less extreme degrees of competition are always taking place, since human cultures are seldom totally isolated for too long. Thus we find within populations that are larger than a single religious culture that some religions may be waxing and others waning while the total population continues to flourish if it finds ways to combine elements of the various religions in suitable ways. It can be noted that this is analogous to genetic recombinations in sexually reproducing organic populations. From this it can be seen that in a single large society, especially a worldwide society, a certain degree of pluralism of religions is healthy.

The above picture of the selection of religious cultures by the ultimate reality that judges all things gives us grounds for respecting any living religious tradition and for suspecting it may contain significant truth for human living, even if it happens to be alien to our ways of understanding.

It also gives us grounds for supposing that any religions that fail to adopt the mythology or symbol system of the contemporary sciences for communicating their messages will likely fail, even if their message is on the whole one that would produce an even richer life if it were believed. That such beliefs may have a value is attested to by such facts as the following. A generation or two ago one heard many skeptics nostalgically say: "Oh, if I could only have the faith my grandfather had, what peace of mind or what courage or nobleness I might have!" Today, the younger generation, knowing more the skepticism or insincerity of the religious belief of some of their elders and hence discounting their native religion, often yearn for the meaning and satisfaction that some alien faith, like Islam or Zen Buddhism, might provide. The importance of communication and its symbol systems is recognized by Christian theologians, who have recently become more convinced that one must translate the religious message so that it can be understood by the people to whom one brings it. Unfortunately, not many of them have been realistic enough to see that the religious or God questions should be expressed in terms of the realities of the well-established scientific symbol system or world view.[3]

In any case, the needs for a scientifically based symbol system for religion are increasing and becoming worldwide in the latter half of the twentieth century, even if the response on the part of religious reformers, theologians, and the like has been as yet inadequate. There was a much greater response among religionists, for instance, in eighteenth-century Europe, when the deistic theology sought to conform to the Newtonian and scientific world view of the times. While for good reasons many traditional Christian religious leaders have feared to try again to integrate their message with the scientific symbol system, more radical innovations have been made by nontraditional, often called "secular," reformers who impatiently felt a better more credible faith for life must be created. I have referred to the various psychotherapeutic cults and social utopias which have arisen out of at least alleged application of scientific knowledge to problems of human salvation at the religious level, reflecting both the personal-emotional and the social needs characteristically served by religions. Unfortunately the personal and social needs are not very well integrated for the most part. Even so, there is a possibility that some of these scientific-religious cults may attain sufficient credibility and power to satisfy man's religious needs before a reformation arises in some of the traditional religions to do this.

Possibly this "secular" approach to religion may even consciously and systematically borrow elements of the traditional religions. Mowrer's picture in Chapter V may imply this possibility. On the other hand, certain groups or elements of the various great religious traditions may come out first in the competition to fill the tremendous human need left in the twentieth century by the evaporation of religious convictions in most of the cultures of the world at a time when a meaning and guide for man's basic values is more urgent than ever. The work of the Jesuit paleontologist Teilhard represents a noble effort from the traditional religious side to integrate with the sciences.

Sharp criticism of both the approach by those with primary roots in the sciences and the approach by those with primary roots in traditional religion are needed. Reformations must be stripped of all that is not viable or workable, of all that is not true. Gilkey's Chapter IV is a good example of this criticism of both types of reformation: the scientific myth type, which is alleged to be neither scientific nor religious enough, and the Teilhardian type, which is also alleged not to be scientific or religious enough.

The Cornerstone for Human Values

Pluralism and diversity, which are needed within limits, can become lethal if increased too far. This is true in the interbreeding gene pool as well as in cultures and religions. In the twentieth century, diversity may have reached beyond the point of the milder disruptions of the first two world wars to a point of potential lethality. Pressing upon the minds of more and more people as the most critical need of our times is the urgency for some reformed symbol system with the power to transform human behavior from its present patterns of self-centered indulgence, apathy, isolation, confusion, and frustration. These present patterns lead to individual and social instability and a possibly lethal lack of sufficient motivation to serve the now complexly interdependent needs of the total world community. This need for world community, for some degree of common concern, for cooperative services in a highly interacting world population, is also strongly reflected by Schilling in Chapter III and Sinsheimer in Chapter VI. While Schilling seems to feel that religious or cultural reformation and renewal will do the job, Sinsheimer is doubtful. He suggests that culture has been failing to do it, and that this failure may be explained by the inadequacy of the human genotype to allow enough altruism and vision. He therefore suggests that we may have to alter the gene pool to make better men. But he does not explain how any present human culture will allow the required changes to be made, nor does he say exactly what is required or how to do it. It is difficult enough to get existing cultures to allow us even to restrain the size of the population, to say nothing about altering its character. Nevertheless, I believe Sinsheimer is correct in suggesting we are on the threshold of the technical capacity to engineer the human genotype, that continued advance and survival may even require it, and that it is none too soon to begin asking what would be good, that is, what would yield optimal life.

While it is true that we do not today have the advanced technology to restructure chemically the details of the chemical information in the human genotypes, any more than in 1940 we had the technology to take a trip to the moon, it is my opinion that the theory and instruments for chemical manipulation of the genotype are in a similar state today as were the theory and instruments for moon trips in 1940. By the year 2000 surprising things may be possible. I make a few notes on salvation by the genotype or the pool of possible genotypes.

In the first place, the human genotype has been under process of change for the past couple of billion years. During the past few thousand years man has increasingly been entering into this selective process himself at a conscious level even though his conscious vision is not always wisely informed. For instance, the late geneticist H. J. Muller[4] and many others have pointed out that modern medicine, in being helpful in preserving people with diseases having a genetic base, is at the same time allowing those who are preserved to breed as well as to live. In procreating, these people are increasing the "genetic load" of humanity, the proportion of the population who will be afflicted by these diseases.

In the second place, this slow reformation of the gene pool by conscious programs of breeding can be used for desirable purposes, provided people agree on what is desirable and are motivated sufficiently to bring it about. Much could be done in a few generations by breeding alone, without the new synthetic technology of "manufacturing" new, nonaccidentally produced genotypes. But knowing what to breed requires a cultural reformation before one could start on a reformation of the gene pool. We still cannot escape the necessity for some kind of cultural reformation prior even to the old-fashioned manipulation of the gene pool by breeding. Cultural reformation is the method that seems to be felt adequate by Schilling and Mowrer. Schilling seems to me to be saying that revitalization and reformation of traditional religion would be the best approach to cultural reform. Mowrer would seem to be saying that a sort of scientific humanism would be a possible way to reform human culture and behavior patterns.

Thirdly, if we apply the new technological powers to synthesize novel or better human genotypes, we must recognize that it is still not man who makes the final decision, the final judgment as to what can be done or what is better. That is made by a system of reality or power superior to man. Man can make something that will be selected or allowed by that reality only when he makes it to accord with the "judgment" or "will" or nature of what that reality will allow to survive. The sciences have made clearer than the Biblical literature that the way to life is very straight and narrow. Most of the possible behaviors and systems are unstable, inviable. Only a very limited few are even temporarily stable.

In religious language I am saying for genetic engineering what Gilkey said in concluding Chapter IV: "for unless the Lord builds the house, the builders do labor in vain." It is interesting to note that Charles Darwin said something very similar: that the builder of living species is natural selection.[5] Any attempts at adaptation that do not correspond with what nature (the total nature of the situation) says is viable will be in vain.

For those familiar with it, natural selection is today's symbol for the man-transcending power or reality that creates and determines man's destiny. While it is true that man can create (both by chance and conscious selection) new living species, he cannot do this unless what he does conforms to nature's requirements. If nature's requirements are met by good luck or chance or by grace of unconscious genetic or cultural information, man can be successfully creative in solving life's problems. If he is to be creative consciously, with some purpose in mind, the rules are still the same: if he is to be successful, he must do only those things which nature will permit. If he seeks to fly or to create new life, he must first fulfill the requirements of the environment, of the nature of the situation in the real world. It is only by first being obedient to what nature requires that he can succeed at all.

Thus, if man is to build a better human genotype (and the same is true for culture type), he must build it in accordance with whatever the realities involved require for it to be successful. He is not free to build anything he might happen to dream or wish. It is only to the degree that his wishes conform to what nature decrees that it is possible for man to succeed. Fortunately, his genotype and culture type may have incarnated in him much of this wisdom selected from nature over millions or billions of years. All man's new achievements under scientific technology are of the same sort, as any thoughtful and knowledgeable man knows. It is by incorporating the requirements of nature that human, conscious, synthetic technology is allowed to perform its miracles. Man has superior powers only to the degree that he incarnates nature's laws and conditions.

The question now facing man, if he would improve his genotype, is to know what in fact nature will require. For anything so complex as the human genotype—which must provide viable information for such a complex system as man, living in an environment so complex as this world with all its varieties of other creatures (human and nonhuman), and with all the other existing and probable conditions of life—this task of knowing what is a better genotype or better gene pool than we now have is incredibly great. Few geneticists believe that we can really do much to improve the human gene pool.[6] It would seem that we may have to continue to suffer the method of progress by trials and errors, as we have in the past, unless we could gather the tremendous amount of information necessary for conscious design of viable genotypes as complex as those of man.

I shall mention one rather critical problem, that of a genetic limitation of altruistic behavior possibly imposed by past and present operations of selection in our species. To remove this limitation may require socially directed natural selection. It has been argued that mammals cannot be selected for self-sacrificial altruism the way the social insects have been. This hinges on the technical fact that in insect societies the whole society is generated by a common zygote, and the social differentiation comes from variation of management of the developing phenotypes, and since there is only one zygote involved there is no genetic selection against those insect castes which give up their lives for the welfare of the total society. In mammalian species and man this has not been the case. The youths whose lives are lost in saving their companions contribute less of their genes to the future gene pool than do those who look out for number one first.[7] Possibly a culturally (socially) controlled production and selection of genotypes could produce men who could happily be as altruistic and cooperative as are members of insect societies. Possibly the new Spaceship Earth—with billions of closely interacting people, critically dependent on highly faithful and specialized mutual services—will require a devotion as strong as that for which insect societies have been naturally selected. We have to examine very carefully whether the present gene pool will allow cultural evolution to move farther toward interdependence without tragic disasters.

It is possible that another area of technology, computers, which I mentioned in Chapter II, may be of some help to us here. In the next millennium, and possibly in the twenty-first century, we may be able to have computers (much of whose own programming they will be doing themselves with the aid of natural selection better than can we) which will be able to advise us how to construct some significant improvements in the human gene pool. I think Sinsheimer is right in his vision that we stand on the threshold of being able to improve our genetic structure by a technological synthesis of DNA information. Perhaps a conjunction of human cultural evolution in the form of computers and this other element of human cultural evolution in the form of genetic technology can produce fantastically better men— angels or minor gods if you will. But the interesting point in the above statement is that it is human culture that is the source of this genetic improvement, not the genes themselves apart from culture, but culture. The genetic and computer technologies as well as the information as to what is a better genotype are all elements of culturally transmitted information in society.

Moreover, if we look again for a moment at the role of computers, it may be that the next evolutionary emergence of great significance will not be better humans through better genotypes, but a new and better kind of life not involving deoxyribonucleic acid blueprints and amino acid building blocks at all. I mentioned briefly this potential of computer technology at the end of the first section of Chapter II. If computers could design a better human genotype, they would already be better than *Homo;* so

why should they try to design better men? Another way of looking at this is to ask, Why should men try to design better worms?

Again, the primary point that I would insist on here is not so
much which technology or just how life will be improved, but
on the clear necessity that, whatever the route, the ultimate requirement is that "unless the Lord builds the house, the builders
do labor in vain." The potential new kingdom of life made up
of self-replicating and rapidly evolving computers, as well as
supermen from a culturally synthesized, superhuman genotype,
all serve the same God—in the language of science, the same
ultimate necessities or laws and boundary conditions imposed by
nature, the ultimate reality.

Thus the God concept becomes for me the cornerstone for
human and all other values. If the builders reject it, their whole
edifice will crumble. I see the scientific myths of lawful cosmic
evolution, such as the one by Shapley that I quoted in Chapter
VIII, a nature that selects and ordains human destiny and all
other destiny, as essentially a confirmation of the central message
of the religions of the world, a message that I believe will be
revitalized in the twenty-first century in a universal symbol system coherent with the sciences. This scientific myth or hypothesis
or conviction is a matter of deep faith that experience has everywhere been confirming—the faith that all events in the cosmos
may be found to be parts of a single whole, operating according
to universal laws. We now know these laws have been revealed
to man in remoter times by his genotype, more recently in his
unconsciously or semiconsciously evolved culture types, and still
more recently as a result of his largely conscious scientific searching. I see this picture of man as the creature of the sovereign
whole to be consonant with much of the religious traditions, and
I see little significant problem in translating the symbol systems
of these religions into the symbol system or language of contemporary science.

I now return to some problems of the conscious and scientific
generation of a better culture type, a culture type hopefully able
to "express" itself in higher, nobler, richer, ultimately more viable
human values.

How Can Scientific-Symbol Theology
Save Souls and Societies?

The integration of the religious symbols of gods into the scientific symbols of the sovereign powers will have the advantage that it will bring the various religious traditions into a common understanding and a more unified and common system of values, since the values would stem from and be expressed in terms of the increasingly single or monistic picture of the sovereign reality from the sciences in which all men are coming to believe. This single sovereign reality is represented in the picture presented by Shapley from which I quoted in Chapter VIII. Such a common, worldwide faith is necessary if we are to be so closely interrelated, interactive, and interdependent in a now small, crowded, and easily disrupted spaceship.

I find no comparable power for rapid transcultural integration and no such common ground of symbols and understanding to exist among the traditional religions by themselves. If we had time for the old, slow-moving, cultural evolution of the pre-scientific era, I am sure that eventually one of the religions or some reasonably unified abstraction from several or all of them would eventually evolve to make a common value culture for a more slowly attained technology that enables all men to live in one interdependent society. But we do not have time for that, any more than a starving population has time to wait for a new crop next summer. We have to act quickly. The new religious value system has to be here very shortly or total societies as well as many individual psyches may be disintegrated.

I have mentioned the possibility of a religion synthesized by the application of the sciences without using any significant models from traditional religious cultures. Mowrer's program of a kind of scientific humanism borrows a bit from traditional religious technology in terms of the small mutual-help groups. However, here in Chapter V he seems to be rejecting the cornerstone from traditional religion which I find most essential from the perspective of both religion and science. I fancy that he is led to this position partly because a psychologist is less likely than physical and biological scientists to see and be impressed with the universality and dominance of nature as selector of life, including human cultural life. I have to admit, however, that it is from two other distinguished psychologists that I have been finding significant confirmations of the theory of natural selection's operation to establish human cultures. It also may be that Mowrer's resistance to the God concept is that he has been thinking of it in its more restricted formulations. In any case, from my scientific more than from my religious background, I find it imperative for man's salvation that he acknowledge the reality of the infinitely superior power that directs his personal destiny and that of the whole cosmos. And my scientific study and analysis of religion and of theological and scientific language have led me to conclude that it is proper to say this is a translation of the term "god."

I do not mean to disagree with either Mowrer or Sinsheimer in their view that man can and must do something to advance his own salvation. There is no question about this. Even in the religious traditions with a predestination theology, there has been no question but what man has duties and is required to do all he can, even though ultimately it is the Lord who elects or selects. This is so close to natural selection doctrine that I am surprised that more has not been made of it. But what I am disagreeing with is the view that man makes his own values, that he, independently of the realities of *nature,* can do what he wants, or that he is in charge of his own evolution or destiny, or that he now, because of science or technology or cultural evolution, is suddenly free from the forces that for billions of years have determined his development, or that what he wants or wishes is necessarily good or possible. All these notions fail to acknowledge even an elementary notion of natural selection: that our genetically programmed conscious wishes and wants (e.g., sex) have themselves been established by natural selection. This does not guarantee that they will adequately motivate life in future circumstances—only that they have up to now. The settings of these goals, values, or norms in the complex network of negative feedback homeostats of human life systems have been determined in the large by natural selection of the genotype and the culture type. Whenever man or accident turns them to a different setting, unless it is one that the *nature* of the total circumstances will admit as fulfilling the very straight and narrow requirements for a life system, that is, unless *nature* approves or selects, this would be the end of that line.

There may be many features that people will not like about a scientifically grounded theology of the ultimate determinants of human destiny. If they persist in stubbornly refusing to recognize the objective source that determines their values and insist on doing what they personally or collectively happen to wish, when this is different from what the total *nature* of the situation or what that Lord requires, there is then no help for them. They will simply cease to be, not only as individuals, but as a type; for that type is inviable by definition in these circumstances. Any one who chooses death rather than life may do so, and he and his line will be granted their choice. They will cease to be. Natural selection is essentially the same for genotypes and culture types as it is for a boy trying to balance on a railroad track. If he fails to do what nature requires, he will fail. Selection for life is essentially this in principle, except it is vastly more complex. But, in either case, man cannot successfully defy what *nature* requires.

What is salvation in this picture, then? Salvation here, strangely enough, is not the resignation that many wish to suggest when you tell them that the Lord's laws cannot be changed and that man's life is ordained. People tend to throw up their hands or shrug their shoulders and say, Then what is the use of my trying to do anything? Determinism (scientific or theological) takes out all the motivation and meaning of my life, all the freedom. But this is not so if one takes a careful look at what the sciences have been revealing about the nature of life and its evolution. Every creature is constantly seeking new and better adjustments. The progress of life's development from molecules to men, and from infants to men, is the result of constant trials in search of what the Lord ordains. It is written in our very genes that we, who are in so large part graced with life because of what they program for us, must constantly seek to adapt ourselves in new and better ways to the requirements laid down by the larger nature or Lord for the further development or evolution of life. Those individuals and species of life who do not constantly seek to adapt to the sovereign requirements of what must be done to remain in being simply are among those who once were and no longer are.

We cannot in this book develop a scientifically grounded theology. That is another and larger task. I have mentioned some brief sketches of scientifically grounded God talk because I believe that this is central to the problem of prophecy for human values in the twenty-first century. My prophecy, then, is that God talk, talk about the supreme determiner of human destiny, will in the next century increasingly be fostered by the scientific community. Probably some pioneers from all the major religious traditions will also find in the new scientific revelations about the determiner of human destiny a strong faith in the sovereignty of the ultimate reality by whatever name their tradition has called it. As the various religious traditions more and more integrate with, or translate their local symbol systems into, the universal symbol systems of a worldwide scientific-technological culture, religions will be revitalized as well as somewhat reformed, the more adequately to guide man in his choices of right versus wrong, his value choices.

In this view, religion, together with its theoretical myths or hypotheses in theology, is not a phase of culture that is passing away at the end of the second millennium. It is as permanent a part of human life as language. What is happening is that we are coming to speak a new language, a single common language, that is, to conceive of or see the world in the symbols of modern science rather than in the symbols (languages) of earlier times. We can all now see the picture of the one world which is our spaceship circling the sun. This is the symbol of our coming common culture. It is also the symbol of the depth of the scientific perspectives that are continually unveiling ever further the nature of our ultimate sources and our requirements as participants in the creation story. Through these revelations we can revivify and extend the noblest visions of earlier prophets to give ourselves and our fellowmen greater hope and greater life.

Salvation (the maintenance and advancement of the quality of life for men), I suspect, is going to depend more immediately on the evolution of culture type than of genotype. While we shall probably have the possibility of a technological acceleration of the evolution of human genotypes, they will come under the direction of cultural evolution because technology is cultural. Culture, and more especially scientific culture, has the capacity more quickly to find more adequate responses to what nature requires for life than could learning by genetic trials. Genetic technology is thus primarily a taking over of genetic change or mutation by culture. Here the culture selects the genotype rather than that the genes make possible a better culture. But in reality both are involved and selected together since culture is itself selected by the same realities of the nature of things that selects the gene. It is the same nature that reinforces or selects the learning of viable adaptations or ways of life regardless of the level of advancement of the ways of generating novel trials or response patterns. Therefore, central for the effectiveness of the more rapid advance of cultural evolution under science, or genetic evolution by genetic technology, is the recognition that the ultimate selector and determiner of the shape of things is nature in the large sense I have noted above, nature as the total system of all things in its dynamic flow from one state to another under invariant laws.

I suspect that man's present genetic boundaries will not prevent him from learning culturally fast enough what are his requirements if he is to adapt to the realities of his new world community. He can learn now, as he did through his religious cultures in the past, that it is his pleasure as well as his necessity to interact as a self-giving servant for the sake of the larger community of man and of the total evolutionary program of the Lord.

With our present genotypes, what is necessary for men to become motivated consciously to meet the higher social requirements of the new age seems to me to be that their culture present them with a clear conviction of what is necessary as defined by the nature of their situation. It is our lack of faith in and commitment to some such system of ideals (goals or values) that is our primary problem. This lack of faith in traditional religious symbols was a first response by people to the scientific world view when it seemed to them to be saying different things from what were presented in the older symbol systems or world views by the traditional religions. But, a deeper look at both science and religion shows them not at cross purposes. As Wallace said: "Religion and science . . . would seem to be the more direct expressions of this organizational instinct."[8]

When theology becomes integrated in the scientific myth or symbol system, then it will be believed as are the other myths of the sciences. The religious myths of the past were in the symbols that were a part of or consonant with the "science" of the time and place. And, if the myth is believed, men will behave as if it were so. If because of science a few men believe man can travel to the moon, then sooner or later many or all of us will cooperate together to soar to the heavens. Scientific faith does allow us to work miracles.

If one of the requirements for our heaven is an orderly, cooperative, closely knit society of a few billion men on Spaceship Earth, the scientific clarification of how to do this will in principle be no more impossible than clarification of how to reach the moon. The technological achievement is similarly possible because of the realism and conviction of the faith that underlies it.

Because of the pressures of a distraught world, I suggest that when the credible new religious myth is born, it will sweep the world rapidly, and it will need to. Man can then enter into an age that is at least as superior to ours as ours is superior to those of 1000 B.C. The reformation could get significantly under way in the decade of the 1970's. But it may not appear until after the new millennium arrives.

Perhaps it is best to conclude my prophecy of a worldwide scientifically based religion in the twenty-first century with a brief statement about its probability. Scientists, as other men throughout all time, must hedge their bets. Men do not have good enough hypotheses or enough facts—in fact we do not even have the mental or computer capacity to handle the facts even if we had them—to make predictions on most matters with 100 percent certainty. Prophecies about human history can have no such certainty.

We have to live with uncertainty, even in the most scientific world. Man's search for certainty is of the essence of his life. This is the search for order, and order he must have or he will not exist. But to hope for complete certainty would be to hope for the end of evolution. The cosmic picture from the sciences suggests that living beings will continue to risk trials with high probabilities of failures and sufferings for a good many billion years yet, maybe indefinitely. Risk of error is the price of progress, of evolution to higher levels. Our religion, like traditional religions, will have to reconcile us to the everlasting quest for certainty in the midst of everlasting uncertainty. In such a context, man needs to and can learn to trust the processes of nature in which he plays his role. While it is essential that we struggle to our utmost to find and do the right, we can be assured, paradoxically it seems, that the sovereign source of life and its evolution upward revealed by the sciences, like the God revealed by ancient religions, will do what it will do. It is what it is. This ultimate judge and selector of what shall persist is not man. It is the *nature,* the *reality,* that defines the righteous as those whose lives or beings it prospers in the end, and that defines the wicked as those whose lives it causes to perish. Human values are set by the natural Lord God Almighty, not by man. For man is as a blade of grass that grows in the day and is gone by night, but the total system of reality or nature reigns forever. Man's privilege and man's only hope is to adapt, to serve the will of the Lord.

Such a vision is not novel except for the conviction with which it may be held in the twentieth century by one who finds it revealed in the scientific myth of creation. Such a vision may allow one to try to bring about a reformation of theology in the light of the sciences without total assurance that it will come in time, or that it will come at all.

Our task forever is to discern the will of the Most High and then to seek to fulfill it, forever confessing our errors and reforming our ways.

NOTES

1. E.g., Anthony F. C. Wallace, *Religion: An Anthropological View* (Random House, Inc., 1966), or Arnold Toynbee, *An Historian's Approach to Religion* (Oxford University Press, Inc., 1956).

2. Donald T. Campbell, "Variation and Selective Retention in Socio-Cultural Evolution," *General Systems,* Vol. 14 (1969), pp. 69–85.

3. Philip Hefner, "The Relocation of the God-Question," *Zygon, Journal of Religion and Science,* Vol. V, No. 1 (March, 1970), pp. 5–17, cf. esp. p. 17.

4. Hermann Joseph Muller, "Should We Weaken or Strengthen Our Genetic Heritage?" in Hudson Hoagland and Ralph Burhoe (eds.), *Evolution and Man's Progress* (Columbia University Press, 1962).

5. Cf. reference in L. Charles Birch, *Nature and God* (The Westminster Press, 1965), p. 42.

6. See, for example, James F. Crow, "Mechanisms and Trends in Human Evolution," in Hoagland and Burhoe (eds.), *op. cit.,* pp. 6–21.

7. Cf. George C. Williams, *Adaptation and Natural Selection: A Critique of Some Current Evolutionary Thought* (Princeton University Press, 1966).

8. See Anthony F. C. Wallace's quotation in Chapter VII.